SHAKESPEARE'S ITALIAN SETTINGS AND PLAYS

Shakespeare's Italian Settings and Plays

Murray J. Levith
Professor of English
Skidmore College, New York

St. Martin's Press   New York

© Murray J. Levith, 1989

All rights reserved. For information, write:
Scholarly & Reference Division,
St. Martin's Press, Inc., 175 Fifth Avenue, New York, NY 10010

First published in the United States of America in 1989

Printed in Hong Kong

ISBN 0-312-00911-9

Library of Congress Cataloging-in-Publication Data
Levith, Murray J.
Shakespeare's Italian settings and plays/Murray J. Levith.
p.   cm.
Bibliography: p.
Includes index.
ISBN 0-312-00911-9: $29.95
1. Shakespeare, William, 1564–1616—Knowledge—Italy.
2. Shakespeare, William, 1564–1616—Settings.   3. Italy in literature.   I. Title.
PR3069.18L48   1989
822.3'3—dc19
87-21277
CIP

For Tina

Contents

List of Plates	viii
Preface	ix
1 Illyria, Italia, Englandia	1
2 Venice	12
A *The Merchant of Venice*	18
B *Othello*	29
3 The Terra Firma	40
A *The Taming of the Shrew*	46
B *Romeo and Juliet*	54
C *The Two Gentlemen of Verona*	60
4 Beyond the Signory	65
A *All's Well That Ends Well*	70
B *Much Ado About Nothing*	76
C *The Tempest*	82
5 The Undiscovered Country	87
Notes	91
Index	102

List of Plates

1a Coryat and courtesan. From Thomas Coryat, *Coryat's Crudities*, 1611.
 b Venetian courtesan wearing chapineys. From Pietro Bertelli, *Diversarum nationum habitus*, vol. 1, 1594.
2 'The Description of Venice'. From Fynes Moryson, *An Itinerary*, 1617.
3 Rialto Bridge. From Pietro Bertelli, *Diversarum nationum habitus*, vol. 3, 1596.
4a Venetian merchant.
 b Noble moor.
 From Cesare Vecellio, *Degli habiti antichi et moderni*, 1590.
5 Sword and dagger. From George Silver, *Paradoxes of Defence*, 1599.
6 Milan. From Georg Braun, *Civitates orbis terrarum*, 1572.
7a Florence. From Pietro Bertelli, *Theatrum urbium Italicarum*, 1599.
 b Siena. From Georg Braun, *Civitates orbis terrarum*, 1572.
8 'The Battle of Lepanto'. Anonymous artist.

'The Battle of Lepanto' is reproduced with permission of the National Maritime Museum, Greenwich. All other plates are reproduced with permission of The Folger Shakespeare Library, Washington, D.C.

Preface

Heminge and Condell listed the plays they collected according to genre, and from the First Folio onward there has been a tendency to group Shakespeare's plays in one way or another. Renaissance Italy was a favourite locale for Shakespeare, and this study brings together his non-classical Italian plays. I consider eight works of various genres, written throughout the dramatist's career, in the context of their settings.

The book is organized into five sections. Chapter 1 is introductory. Chapters 2 to 4 are arranged first to discuss from an English perspective the specific geographical area used by Shakespeare in a group of plays, then to examine the plays located there. Thus, Chapter 2 is about Venice and the Venetian plays, Chapter 3 about the so-called *terra firma* (territories on the Italian mainland subject to the State of Venice) and plays set in those cities, and Chapter 4 about areas beyond the Signory and plays so located. Chapter 5, the final section, reviews opinion as to whether or not Shakespeare visited Italy.

My approach to the plays may seem somewhat eclectic, since only those issues that grow out of setting are explored. In certain works, these issues are decidedly more central than in others. Some plays, therefore, receive more expansive attention.

All quotations are from *The Riverside Shakespeare* (Boston: Houghton Mifflin, 1974), G. Blakemore Evans textual editor. For clarity, I have omitted the brackets Evans uses for questionable readings. My brackets indicate insertions.

Skidmore College granted me a sabbatical leave to draft my manuscript, and I received three additional grants toward the realization of this book from the Skidmore Faculty Committee on Research Grants. As always, Dean of Faculty Eric Weller has been encouraging and supportive in every possible way.

The collections of many libraries in the US and abroad were used for research, but the Folger Shakespeare Library, the New York State Library, and the State University of New York at Albany Library were especially forthcoming with needed books and microfilm. The late Gloria Moore, inter-library loan librarian at Skidmore, provided invaluable assistance in helping locate obscure material. Librarians Alvin Gamage, Barbara Smith, Judith Reese, and Rosemary Del Vecchio were there when I needed them, as was Reference Assistant Marilyn Sheffer.

At an early stage of my work, the Snow Library, Orleans, Massachusetts, gave me the opportunity to present some of my ideas as a part of their winter lecture series. More recently, drafts of sections of this material were offered at Iowa State University, Florida Atlantic University, New College (University of South Florida), and West Virginia University.

All of my Shakespeare students helped along the way by discussing in and writing for my classes. Student Assistants Adah Franklin, Maureen Bouley, Brian Downing, and Clark Matthews typed, xeroxed, checked, proofed, and did other painstaking detail work. I especially wish to thank Clark Matthews for his highly professional computer expertise. Amy Shore and Susan Stein assisted with the Index. Debbie Mar helped with final proofreading.

Dr Stanley Wells and Mr Robert Stein read a preliminary draft. My colleague Dr Phillip J. West read the final manuscript, and saved me from several embarrassments.

Finally, and most importantly, loving thanks to Nathaniel and Willy who tolerated their daddy's 'homework' (sometimes), and Tina who, as usual, endured it all.

Qufu Normal University
Shandong Province
The People's Republic of China

1
Illyria, Italia, Englandia

> Italy worthily called the Queene of Nations, can never be sufficiently praised, being most happy in the sweete Ayre, the most fruitfull and pleasant fields, warme sunny hils, hurtlesse thickets, shaddowing groves, Havens of the Sea, watering brookes, baths, wine, and oyle for delight, and most safe forts or defenses as well of the Sea as of the Alpes.
>
> Fynes Moryson

> It hath a very temperate and wholesome air, fertile fields, pleasant hills, batful pastures, shadowing woods, plenty of all kind of trees and groves, abundance of corn, vines, and olives, good wools, fair cattle, and so many springs, fountains, lakes, rivers, and havens that it is an open lap to receive the trade of all countries; and, as it were to offer all men help, it seemeth willingly to put itself into the sea.
>
> William Thomas

> O Italie, the Academie of man-slaughter, the sporting place of murther, the Apothecary-shop of poyson for all Nations: how many kind of weapons hast thou invented for malice?
>
> Thomas Nashe

Like an American on a one week tour of all of Europe, when Viola comes ashore in the second scene of *Twelfth Night*, she wants to know where she is: 'What country, friends, is this?' (I,ii,1). And the captain assures her, 'This is Illyria, lady' (I,ii,2). Editors dutifully note that Shakespeare takes his place name from a favourite sourcebook, Golding's Ovid, and that Illyria is located in present-day Yugoslavia. Nevertheless, all would also agree that the feel and ambience of Orsino's dukedom of music and love is decidedly Italian – like the settings for a goodly number of other Shakespeare plays.

The beginning of the Elizabethan dramatic fashion for locating plays in more or less contemporary (that is, not classical) Italy is usually dated from George Gascoigne's *Supposes* and the tragedy *Gismund of Salerne*.[1] Gascoigne's drama, staged at Gray's Inn in 1566, is a source for both *The Comedy of Errors* and *The Taming of the Shrew*. An adaptation of Ariosto's *I Suppositi*, it is perhaps the first English comedy based on an Italian play.[2] Roughly two years after *Supposes*, *Gismund of Salerne*, a collaborative effort by five writers, was produced at the Inner Temple. It is thought to be the first English tragedy based on an Italian novella tale.[3]

From this beginning, of course, came a veritable flood of Renaissance English plays set in Italy. The two parts of Thomas Dekker's *The Honest Whore* are set in Milan, Ben Jonson's *Volpone* in Venice, John Marston's *The Malcontent* in Genoa, George Chapman's *All Fools* in Florence, Beaumont and Fletcher's *Philaster* in Sicily; and there is Tourneur's *The Revenger's Tragedy*, Massinger, Ford, John Webster's great plays – the list might go on and on.

Throughout his career Shakespeare returns again and again to Italian settings for all genres of plays. The early tragedy *Romeo and Juliet* is set in Verona and Mantua, and the first act of *Othello* takes place in Venice. Five comedies – two early, two middle, and a problem play – are located either partly or wholly in Italy: *The Taming of the Shrew* in Padua and the neighbourhood of Verona; *The Two Gentlemen of Verona* in Milan, Verona, and a forest near Mantua; *The Merchant of Venice* in Venice and 'Belmont'; *Much Ado About Nothing* in Messina; and *All's Well That Ends Well* in or about Florence in nine scenes. *The Tempest* is set on an unnamed island, but the ruling families of Milan and Naples people it. Another romance, *The Winter's Tale*, is located partly in ancient Sicilia, yet jealousy associated with contemporary Italy motivates the action of the play, Italianate court intrigue is in evidence, and a supposed statue by Julio Romano, an actual Italian artist (d. 1546), is displayed. One of the settings for *Cymbeline* is an ancient Rome having here and there the feel of a Jacobean place. Imogen refers to 'That drug-damn'd Italy' (III,iv,15), complete with 'stews' (I,vi,152), where 'Some jay' (III,iv,49), 'Some Roman courtezan' (III,iv,123) might pervert her husband. The tempter is rather, to be sure, the 'bold Jachimo, / Sienna's brother' (IV,ii,340–1), a recognizably conventional 'false Italian / (as poisonous tongu'd as handed)' (III,ii,4–5). The wager plot of *Cymbeline* perhaps goes back to Boccaccio's *Decameron* (ninth novel, second day) or to *Frederyke of Jennen* [Genoa], but in any case it derives ultimately from an Italian story.[4]

Even plays Shakespeare does not set in Italy sometimes have

Italian sources and strong Italian flavours. *Twelfth Night* in part seems similar to the play *Gl'Ingannati*, whose prologue contains the phrase 'la notte di beffana', where some think Shakespeare found his 'twelfth night' title.[5] Shakespeare's more immediate source is generally conceded to be Barnabe Riche's Apolonius and Silla narrative (in *Riche his Farewell to Militarie Profession*), and Riche, in turn, received his story from, among others, Matteo Bandello.[6] The sentimental tone of *Twelfth Night* has been compared with the Italian entertainment *Il Sacrificio*, which includes in its cast one Agnol Malevolti, a name suggesting Malvolio.[7] *As You Like It* recalls pastoral drama like Tasso's *Aminta* (1572–3) and Guarini's *Il Pastor Fido* (published 1589–90).[8] Shakespeare copies Thomas Lodge's *Rosalynde*, and Lodge earlier found inspiration in Jacapo Sannazaro's *L'Arcadia*.[9]

Measure for Measure is set in Vienna, but like *Othello* its main plot is derived from Giraldi Cinthio's *Hecatommithi*. Shakespeare changed Cinthio's names, perhaps to make them more stereotypically Italian for his English audience: Juriste becomes Angelo, Epitia becomes Isabella, Vico becomes Claudio. Cinthio's Austrian action as Shakespeare's – with nuns and friars, fornication and a bed trick, a corrupt judge, a disguised ruler – may well have been located in Italy. Just as *Measure for Measure*, Hamlet's 'Mouse-trap' is also set in Vienna, and the characters' names and actions are again clearly Italian. The duke's name is Gonzago (similar to Gonzaga, the family name of Mantuan dukes) and his wife is Baptista. The plot concerns murder by poison to satisfy selfish ambition. Hamlet himself tells of the drama's Italian source: 'the story is extant, and written in very choice Italian' (III,ii,262–3).

Though set in Navarre, *Love's Labour's Lost* has recognizable *Commedia dell'arte* figures. Don Adriano de Armado is the braggert soldier, Holofernes the comic pedant, Moth the quick-witted servant, and Sir Nathaniel the clerical parasite. *Commedia* characteristics have been found in a number of Shakespeare plays, even in so English a one as *The Merry Wives of Windsor*.[10]

With all of Shakespeare's attention to Italy and things Italian, it is surprising that over the years only glancing notice has been taken of this aspect of the playwright's work. Among modern scholars, John W. Draper has accomplished the most, presenting his findings in a series of articles ranging from 'Some Details of Italian Local Colour in "Othello"', to 'Shakespeare and Florence and the Florentines', 'Shakespeare and the Doge of Venice', and 'Shakespeare and the

Lombard Cities'.[11] In yet another essay, 'Shakespeare and the Conversatione', Draper writes about manifestations of a formal and mannered Italian rhetorical convention in the plays.[12] As a whole, Draper's work asks what Shakespeare might have known about various Italian regions, customs, traditions, and governments.

The late Mario Praz's 'Shakespeare's Italy' is the most ambitious single piece written on its subject.[13] Reviewing relevant background and past criticism first, Praz next makes 'a rapid survey' of Shakespeare's Italian plays, emphasizing one thing or another as he passes: mistakes in geography, echoes of Italian poetry in *Romeo and Juliet*, local colour in *The Merchant of Venice*, Iago's motivation, political intrigue in *The Tempest*. He concludes with speculation about 'the way in which Shakespeare may have got acquainted with Italian things'. While Praz's essay is admittedly a generalized overview, it highlights relevant areas ripe for further investigation.

Another abbreviated discussion from a different angle is provided by A. C. Partridge in 'Shakespeare and Italy'.[14] Partridge sees Shakespeare as part of a rising wave of 'cosmopolitanism' in Renaissance England, with interest in Italian humanism, education, language, art, and culture generally. He reminds us of the influential Florio family in England, who may have fuelled Shakespeare's interest in Italy and taught him about the country. Like other scholars, Partridge wonders if Shakespeare visited Italy. Brief paragraphs on the influence of the Italian comic, tragic, and poetic traditions, with some discussion of Machiavelli, round out the essay.

Finally, G. H. McWilliams gave his inaugural lecture as Professor of Italian in the University of Leicester on 'Shakespeare's Italy Revisited'.[15] Interesting because it is from the perspective of a translator and scholar of Italian literature, it again addresses the question of 'Shakespeare's knowledge of Italy', but also considers as well 'those Italian authors, chiefly of the fourteenth and sixteenth centuries, to whom he was chiefly indebted'.

Shakespeare's Italian plays were written against a background of intense English interest in Italy. This interest manifested itself in travel to the country, learning the Italian language, translating and being influenced by Italian books, and copying Italian fashions and culture. For Renaissance Englishmen Italy was an exotic place, a fabled land. On the one hand, it was the home of Machiavelli and the Pope; on the other, it was thought the most advanced civilization of the time, the most progressive society. In politics and warfare, science and technology, finance, banking and commerce, art, music, and literature, Italy was the leader. Queen Elizabeth and many of her courtiers (the Earl of Southampton, Shakespeare's patron, for example) knew Italian. Italians visited the court regularly. Alfonso Ferrabosco, from Bologna, was Court Musician to Elizabeth between 1562 and 1578, and other members of his family succeeded him in the position. Petruccio Ubaldini came to England as early as 1545, married an Englishwoman, perhaps served the Queen on the continent for a time, and died in England. *Twelfth Night* may have been written in 1601 expressly for the visit of Don Virginio Orsino, Duke of Bracciano.[16] Marriage proposals for King James' children included ones from Venice and Tuscany. One Ottaviano Lotti spent a number of years in England promoting a marriage between an Italian princess and the Prince of Wales.

Travel to Italy from England began in earnest just after the middle of the sixteenth century and did not slow down until after 1630. The tourists included all kinds – students and merchants, even vagabonds, but especially courtiers. During Elizabeth's reign, a trip to Italy was thought necessary for rounding out a gentleman's education. Many young men, often in the company of guardian tutors, went abroad. In *As You Like It* Jaques tells Rosalind that it is 'the sundry contemplation of my travels' that makes him melancholy (IV,i,17–20). Rosalind dismisses the affected Jaques curtly, calling upon the clichéd image of the English traveller bored with provincial life at home now that he has been to the continent: 'Monsieur Traveller', she says, 'look you lisp and wear strange suits; disable all the benefits of your own country; be out of love with your nativity, and almost chide God for making you that countenance you are; or I will scarce think you have swam in a gundello' (IV,i,33–8).

Based in part on his own travels as well as research, William Thomas (c. 1507–54) wrote the first history of Italy in English (1549, reprinted 1561).[17] A Welshman, Thomas was probably educated at Oxford. He fled to Venice at about age forty when he was accused of embezzlement by his patron Sir Anthony Brown. Thomas stayed in Italy for three years, and his travel while there was extensive. In addition to Venice, he visited Padua, Florence, Rome, Naples, and cities in between. Thomas' book consists of first-hand observations of places, customs, society, and summary histories of important Italian cities. The account of Prospero Adorno, the fifteenth-century Duke of Genoa, is considered by some a possible source for

Shakespeare's *The Tempest*.[18] Thomas' *The History of Italy* was influential in encouraging English enthusiasm for Italy, and it stressed the positive. The emphasis was on Italy as a model of refinement: 'the Italian nation . . . seemeth to flourish in civility most of all other at this day'.[19] Because Thomas focused on Italy's appeal, he played down its religious differences with England.

Another important contemporary traveller, however, did not. In *The Scholemaster* (1570) Roger Ascham (1515–68) writes that he too visited Italy, 'but I thanke God, my abode there, was but ix dayes: And yet I sawe in that lit[t]le tyme, in one Citie [Venice], more libertie to sinne than ever I h[e]ard tell of in our noble Citie of London in ix yeare'.[20] Ascham was convinced that the Italians 'have in more reverence, the triumphes of Petrarche: than the Genesis of Moses: They make more account of *Tullies* offices, than *S. Paules* epistles: of a tale in *Bocace*, than a storie of the Bible'.[21] Allow an Englishman to travel in Italy, says Ascham, and he may return '*Italianato, e un diabolo incarnato*'.[22] He may bring home with him, among other things, the Italian religion, 'Papistrie or worse'.[23]

Thomas Coryat (c. 1577–1617) reports a 1608 visit to Italy in *Coryat's Crudities* (1611).[24] His wide-eyed account details everything he saw from forks and umbrellas to the fashion for topless nudity among women. He ate 'fried Frogges'. Coryat even visited a courtesan, though, he assures his reader, for purely academic reasons.

The most balanced view of Italy from the perspective of a traveller of the time is offered by Fynes Moryson (1566–1630).[25] One can mostly agree with E. S. Bates who writes that Moryson's work 'must form the basis of any description of the countries he saw . . . going, as he does, more into detail than anyone else, and being a thoroughly fair-minded, level-headed, and well educated man whose knowledge was the result of experience'.[26] Educated at Cambridge, Moryson apparently sacrificed a church position to gain further education by travel. His journeys took him beyond Italy, and even beyond the Europe of his day. With typical Renaissance bravura, he wished to do 'a sociological survey of the civilised world of his time', in the words of his modern editor.[27] Another scholar thinks it possible that Moryson and Shakespeare knew one another, and that some of the playwright's Italian details may derive from the traveller – even that Moryson, who studied at Wittenberg from 1590–92, might be a model for Hamlet![28]

In any case, the fictional view of Italy that generally prevailed was

Ascham's. It was nurtured by translations of many lurid Italian novellas. Thomas Nashe's Jack Wilton was undoubtedly an *'unfortunate* traveller' because he wound up in Italy. In Nashe's romance, an English Earl who has been banished to Italy asks Jack: 'Countriman, tell me, what is the occasion of thy straying so farre out of *England* to visit this strange Nation? If it bee languages, thou maist learne them at home; nought but lasciviousnesse is to bee learned here.'[29] The Earl tells Jack that young men bring from Italy only

> the art of atheisme, the art of epicurising, the art of whoring, the art of poysoning, the art of Sodomitrie. The onely probable good thing they have to keepe us from utterly condemning it is that it maketh a man an excellent Courtier, a curious carpet knight: which is, by interpretation, a fine close leacher, a glorious hipocrite. It is nowe a privie note amongst the better sort of men, when they would set a singular marke or brand on a notorious villaine, to say, he hath beene in *Italy*.[30]

John Lyly's *Euphues,* which somewhat parallels *The Two Gentlemen of Verona,* offers yet another negative view of Italy, and this was the general fictional view.

It was also the popular dramatic view. The Jacobeans come first to mind, but the Elizabethans as well loved stories and plays with splendorous Italianate palaces, vengeful murders (perhaps by poison), and Antonios lurking behind every arras. The vices of Italy became a dramatic convention, spilling over to Malta, Spanish tragedies, Denmark, or even the England of the chronicle plays. But Italy itself was *the* setting, a place where anything might be presented – irrational jealousy, passionate love, religious corruption, real adventure, horrible violence.

One can observe in Shakespeare something of the popularly imagined Italy. His plays touch usual motifs: jealousy is a theme in *Othello,* political intrigue a focus in *The Tempest,* religion is at issue in *The Merchant of Venice, All's Well That Ends Well* presents Italians at war, Beatrice would have Benedick 'Kill Claudio' to avenge Hero's dishonour in *Much Ado About Nothing,* beautiful women worth wooing against all odds are to be found in *Romeo and Juliet, The Taming of the Shrew, The Two Gentlemen of Verona.* But Shakespeare's treatment of some of the harsher items of Italian lore seems rather polite. Othello is jealous, but he is not a native Italian. The political fencing in *The Tempest* takes place on a remote island, and all ends happily. The religious conflict in *The Merchant of Venice* is overtly between Judaism and Christianity, rather than the expected and more controversial Catholicism and Protestantism (Shakespeare never satirizes obvious corruption in the Roman Church the way Marlowe and Webster do). Bianca in *Othello* is the only courtesan we can find in the Italian plays, and Shakespeare's other women, in addition to possessing honour and beauty, are brave (Juliet), witty (Beatrice), loyal (Julia), strong-willed (Kate), learned (Portia) – rather an attractive lot on the whole.

At first, Italian characters presented in English plays were merely depicted as comic foreigners. But then the Machiavellian stereotype took over, most often in his native Italian setting.[31] This Machiavel became a symbol for what the Renaissance English hated and feared but, at the same time, was fascinated by about Italy. Machiavelli was a devil linked with the Pope and his religion, and he personified power-hungry ruling Italian families like the Borgias. He evolved into a melodramatic stage villain associated with the morality Vice character. The real Machiavelli's work, of course, was misunderstood by the English. Books written by antagonists, some of them with little comprehension of the philosopher's ideas, were more read than Machiavelli himself. *Il Principe* (not published in English until 1640) was viewed as a call for tyranny and repression, rather than as about strategies for effective leadership. Machiavelli was portrayed as an apologist for dictators. And Shakespeare, not knowing much if anything of the real Machiavelli, breathed what was in his English air.

Shakespeare's work contains a quantity of 'Machiavillains'. What is curious, however, is that many of his most Machiavellian characters – Aaron, Regan, Goneril, Bullingbroke, for example – are to be found outside his Italian plays. His British overreachers, such as Richard III and Edmund, especially come to mind, displaying as they do the typical characteristics of ambition, greed, ruthlessness, irreligion, and immorality in serving their own ends. When plotting his crown in *Henry VI, Part 3*, Richard boasts that he will 'set the murtherous Machevil to school' (III,ii,193). Other specific references to Machiavelli appear in *Henry VI, Part 1* (V,iv,74) and in *The Merry Wives of Windsor* (III,i,101). The Bastard's soliloquy on 'commodity' in *King John* is one of a number of typically Machiavellian speeches in Shakespeare. It concludes with the blasphemy: 'Gain, be my lord, for I will worship thee' (II,i,598).

Just as Shakespeare's Machiavellian villains are mostly outside his contemporary Italy, the meaner features associated with the stage country are found in the non-Italian plays. *Titus Andronicus*, for example, set in classical Rome, is a violent and bloody revenge tragedy of rape, murder, maiming, and worse; assassination, court intrigue, and the use of poison are to be found in *Hamlet*; eye gouging and family betrayal in *King Lear*; proverbial Italian-like immorality in *Troilus and Cressida*. Shakespeare's Italian plays, therefore, seem closer to the affirmative picture of Italy forwarded by Thomas and some of the comic romance literature – closer, that is, to Ariosto and Castiglione than the more modern mythic Italy.

All but one of the five major Renaissance Italian power centres are employed by Shakespeare as settings in his plays. Venice and the Venetian *terra firma*, including Padua, Verona, and Mantua just beyond, is his favourite. Milan and Florence are the other two in the north. Messina, a Spanish controlled protectorate like Milan, is his only southern setting. In all but his classical plays Shakespeare avoids Rome, the headquarters of the Papal States. By omitting Rome as a setting, Shakespeare kept controversial Christian religious issues only implicit in some of his plays.

Fynes Moryson observes: 'Touching the Cities of Italy, it is proverbially said [that] . . . Rome [is] the holy, Padua the learned, Venice the Rich, Florence the Beautiful, Milan the great, . . . [and] Naples the Gentile.'[32] 'Individual cities were also associated with specific evils', adds J. W. Stoye: 'Above all Rome was England's danger. In the Elizabethan Protestant's blurred image of the Papal city, Jesuits, assassins, Machiavelli's politics, Venetian Harlotry, the influence of Spanish overlords in Milan and Naples, all seemed constituent elements in a power menacing the life, liberty, and salvation of your Protestant Englishman.'[33] Shakespeare's characters from specific Italian cities have recognizable traits, and not always those with the traditional associations. His Florentine gentlemen, like Cassio, Claudio, and Lucentio (whose hometown is Florence), are mostly well-spoken, courteous, and not especially political, as we might have expected them to be coming from the city of Machiavelli. Bertram fights for Florence as part of his gentlemanly education; Machiavelli, we recall, wrote *The Art of War* as well as *The Prince*. The women from Florence in *All's Well That Ends Well* are honourable. The Venetian milieu of *The Merchant of Venice* and *Othello* suggests sophistication and cosmopolitanism. Jews and Moors are about, Antonio's circle seems very social, the Italian Iago has a name of Spanish origin, Bianca plies her trade here. Othello's insecurity comes in part from believing that Desdemona is one of those 'super-subtle Venetian' women, thus capable of deceiving his simple non-Venetian self. Shakespeare's gentlemen from Verona, Romeo, Petruchio, Proteus, Valentine, all seek wives. Padua, as might be expected, signals learning and wit: Benedick is from Padua, the disguised Portia arrives from this city to plead Antonio's case in court, Lucentio comes to Padua explicitly for education.

Most of Shakespeare's Italian plays are comedies (only two are tragedies), and it is not surprising to find present the inevitable comic conflict between parents and children. Fathers consider daughters difficult: Baptista Minola has his problems with both Bianca and Kate, Leonato believes the charge against Hero and is ready to disown her, Shylock learns that Jessica has run off with his money to marry a Christian. But the tragedies, too, manifest father and daughter conflicts: old Capulet is well-meaning but impossible to Juliet, and Brabantio eventually dies of grief at the mismatch of Desdemona. Fathers dead have planned ahead for daughters living, as in the cases of Helena and Portia. The relationships between fathers and sons are generally happy: in the end Vincentio is satisfied with Lucentio's choice of wife, as is Alonso with Ferdinand's; Petruchio has extended his late father's estate; Old Gobbo helps Launcelot to a better service. There are a number of surrogate fathers for sons in the Italian plays: the King of France for Bertram, Antonio for Bassanio, and Don Pedro for both Claudio and Benedick. The Countess serves Helena as a surrogate mother before she becomes her mother-in-law.

In almost all the dramas set in Italy, learning and education are major themes. Prospero carefully instructs Miranda, but gives up on the hopeless Caliban. Romeo and Juliet both mature while learning that they cannot escape their fate. Kate is tamed and taught by Petruchio, Bertram gains his manhood after rejecting his false tutor, Benedick discovers to his surprise that he wishes to be a married man, Proteus and Valentine find out about love and friendship.

At once the cradle of past civilization and now the newest frontier, Italy surely implied lessons for more than characters in a play – English audiences were also meant to be instructed. An obvious message in *Romeo and Juliet* and *The Tempest* is that factious noble families hamper rule and confuse social and political order. Marrying well and managing an estate wisely is central in a number of plays.

Shakespeare's city settings are vague on specific geography. The Arno in Florence or the Adige in Verona, for example, are never mentioned. And there are few concrete physical details to locate a place. When the Rialto in Venice or St. Gregory's Well near Milan is alluded to, it comes as a surprise. Some of the most famous architectural sights of a city – like the amphitheatre or Roman ruins of Verona – are missing. All we are told usually is that a particular city is old, fair, has walls, gates, citizens. One might conclude from the consistency that this vagueness is purposeful. The settings tend to be evocative but not intrusive – characters and action are kept always in the forefront.

Most importantly Italy serves in part as metaphor for Shakespeare's England – the metropolitan virtues and vices of Italian places are those of the Queen's and King's cities. The unnamed tidal river in Verona is really the Thames of London. Paduan scholars, Florentine courtiers, Venetian villains are types of Englishmen in disguise. There are 'alehouses' not wine cellars in Shakespeare's Italy. The playwright does not even bother to make many of the servants' names Italian – Susan Potpans and Hugh Oatcakes people these plays. The island in *The Tempest* is allegorically the playwright's land.

Thus, when we scratch the surface of Duke Orsino's Illyria in *Twelfth Night*, or indeed the surface of any of the Italian plays, we find Shakespeare's England. Olivia's country house with a waiting gentlewoman, fool, steward, and parasitic relative with friends downstairs is, shall we say, Charlecote Manor. Sir Andrew, Parolles, Tybalt are Englishmen Italianated with dancing back tricks, supposed language fluency, and 'fancy' swordsmanship. Despite his Italian name, Malvolio is recognized as an ambitious upwardly mobile middle-class English Puritan. Sebastian and Antonio plan to lodge at *The Elephant*, a bankside London Inn near the Globe Theatre frequented by Italians.[34]

Viola, then, understandably asks her captain, as we might on a whirlwind trip abroad, what country she has touched when she sets foot on land. Illyria seems Italia, and Italia, to be sure, seems Englandia. Where are we indeed? What country, friends, *is* this?

2
Venice

In *Richard II* the banished Norfolk 'retir'd himself/To Italy, and there at Venice gave/His body to that pleasant country's earth' (IV,i,96–8). The loquacious Holofernes in *Love's Labour's Lost* rhapsodizes, 'as the traveller doth of Venice: *Venechia, Venechia, / Che non te vede, che non te prechia*' (IV,ii,95–8).[1] Shakespeare sets parts of two plays, *The Merchant of Venice* and *Othello*, in the city proper, and much of his other Italian geography lies within the Venetian *terra firma*. Clearly Venice was a special place in the minds of the Renaissance English.

William Thomas is intrigued by the great city's unlikely situation: 'he that beholdeth the place where Venice standeth and would imagine it to be without any building or habitation should say it were the rudest, unmeetest, and unwholesomest place to build upon or to inhabit that were again to be found throughout an whole world'.[2] He adds that despite Venice's unhospitable location, 'no place of all Europe [is] able at this day to compare with that city for number of sumptuous houses, specially for their fronts'.[3] Thomas Coryat similarly notes 'the rarenesse of the situation of Venice' and the 'many sumptuous and magnificent Palaces', but contends modestly that he feels inadequate 'to describe so beautifull, so renowned, so glorious a Virgin'.[4] For Venice is, according to Coryat, 'the most glorious and heavenly shew upon the water that ever mortal eye beheld'.[5]

But Venice was also by reputation, in the words of John Day's 1608 comedy *Humor Out of Breath*, 'the best flesh-shambles in Italy'.[6] As would be expected, Roger Ascham abhorred what he perceived as Venetian immorality and vice, and was especially appalled by what he found out about marriage customs there: 'it is counted good policie, when there be foure or five brethren of one familie, one, onelie to marie: and all the rest, to waulter, with as little shame, in open lecherie, as Swyne do here in the common myre'.[7] Thomas, however, points out sagely that the practice of allowing courtesans reduces the number of legitimate offspring, thereby resulting in clearer claims to family estates. Additionally, courtesan bastards could supply the church.⁸ Even Thomas, though, was taken aback by the way sons were brought up to be 'hail fellows' with their fathers, observing that by 'twenty years of age, . . . [they] knoweth as much lewdness as is possible to be imagined'.⁹ Indeed, Thomas reports, the 'greatest exercise' young men take is to patronize prostitutes.¹⁰ Only in Venice might there be a legal case in which courtesans sued to prevent tennis courts from being built, 'lest it should hinder their trading'.¹¹

Coryat explains the word *courtesan* 'is derived from the Italian word cortesia that signifieth courtesie. Because these kinde of women are said to receive courtesies of their favourites'.¹² Surely they gave some as well! Venetian gentlemen lavished costly jewellery and clothing on their mistresses, who sometimes became quite wealthy. Thomas describes a number of courtesans 'so rich that in a mask, or at the feast of a marriage, or in the shroving time, you shall see them decked with jewels as they were queens'.¹³ Coryat passed a 'Monastery of Augustinian Monkes' between Venice and Murano built by a courtesan ('I have not heard of so religious a worke done by so irreligious a founder in any place of Christendome').¹⁴ Unlike the situation for courtesans in Florence, where they were required to wear yellow veils, Moryson writes, 'In Venice they are free to dwell in any house they can hyre, and in any street whatsoever, and to weare what they list.'¹⁵ What huge tax revenues Venice must receive from her 'Harlotts', speculates Moryson.¹⁶

The beauty of Venetian women and their fashions were proverbial. With quaint diction, Thomas offers that no city can 'compare with Venice for the number of gorgeous dames'.¹⁷ 'The Italyans love fatt and tall wemen,' writes Moryson, 'and for those causes the Venetian wemen are sayd to be Belle di bellito, bianche di calcina, grasse di straccie, alte di legni o zoccole, that is fayre with paynting, white with chalke, fatt with raggs (or stuffed linnen) and high with wood or Pantofles (which many weare a foot or more deepe).'¹⁸ Coryat was fascinated by the fashionable platform footwear called 'chapineys', and observed women balancing on them precariously with the help of servants. He reports seeing one take a nasty fall on the steps of a bridge.¹⁹ Coryat was also excited by the Venetian fashion for bare breasts, though he calls it 'very uncivill and unseemly, especially if the beholder might plainly see them'.²⁰

There were other sophisticated surprises to be encountered in Venice. A citizen might excuse debt by sitting on a special stone with 'naked buttocks three times in some public assembly'.[21] Women were to be seen acting on the public stage.[22] And, for the height of sophistication, Moryson reports as 'not rare' a Venetian on a 'Closestoole . . . talking with his chamber fellowes while they are eating.'[23]

A major international seaport, Venice was one of the truly cosmopolitan cities of Europe, with many nationalities crowding its narrow streets and canals. In the best interests of the economy, its government was necessarily liberal and, in general, religiously tolerant. While the Inquisition was a real and present danger for English Protestants elsewhere in Italy, according to Moryson there was 'no danger . . . at all in the State of Venice to him that can hold his peace, and behave himselfe modestly'.[24] Such men as Henry Parvis, an expatriate English merchant, could set himself up in the city to teach young gentlemen the tricks of international trade.[25] By the last decade of the sixteenth century, there were so many English in Venice that the Pope twice complained loudly about the 'heretics' congesting the city.[26] Before 1603 there was a token diplomat to oversee English tourists, but after this date a full-fledged ambassador, Sir Henry Wotton, from the court of King James. A traveller might even attend Anglican Sunday services at the ambassador's chapel and observe, in Coryat's words, the 'true worship of God in the middest of Popery, superstition, and idolatry'.[27] Nominally Catholic in religion, Venice was anti-papal politically. Rome was a competing power centre.

Since their common fear was Rome and its sometime ally Spain, Venice and England, once antagonists as major sea powers with similar commercial interests and traditions of piracy against one another, were brought together by the close of the sixteenth century. During James' reign, relations between them were mostly cordial. The Venetian republican government was admired because it was perceived as much like the monarchical English – that is, fair and just. Thomas writes of the 'Duke, called after their manner *Doge*, who only (amongst all the rest of the nobility) hath his office immutable for term of life.'[28] Moryson writes that the Venetian Senate 'is most reverent for the grey heads, . . . but for nothing more than their strict observing of Justice'.[29] Shakespeare makes his senates roughly equivalent to the English Parliament, but he is unsure of the interaction of Doge and Senate and evinces little real knowledge of the Venetian system.[30] In the courtroom scene of *The Merchant of Venice*, Shylock taunts the Duke whose hands are tied by the law and thus cannot help Antonio. In *Othello*, the Duke seems weak and silly – at the mercy of a foreign general and his own counsellors. The English monarchy, by implication, with an hereditary queen or king and a wise parliament to advise, was even better than the governmental system that by reputation throughout Europe was best.

Venice was an excellent setting for presenting complex issues. On the one hand, it could be a place of individual freedoms associated with Renaissance social mobility; on the other, it was home to cruel despots who murdered and repressed. Its beautiful women were sometimes wives of questionable virtue, or courtesans of true heart. Exotic strangers with different cultures and costumes mixed freely in the population. For Thomas Coryat, Venice was the 'Jerusalem of Christendom',[31] but it was also nominally Catholic. Venice, thus, could be anything – Italy and not Italy, England, or even 'hell'. The first person Jack Wilton meets in Venice is a panderer, but 'apparalled in all points like a gentleman & having halfe a dosen several languages in his purse'.[32] The immoral and the refined are here juxtaposed. The real Vittoria Corombona came from Gubbio, but Webster makes his character from Venice, 'a city famed throughout Europe for its whores'.[33] Webster's Vittoria is an honourably descended strumpet who is true to her love, and she evokes audience sympathy in *The White Devil*. Marston's *Antonio and Mellida* and *Antonio's Revenge* present Venice as a place containing both weak Andrugio and Antonio, and cruel and hard Piero Sforza. The Duke, in *Antonio's Revenge*, would unite Italy, a good thing if the allegory is applied to England, but he is a tyrant and Marston's audience cheers his defeat.

Based on the report of William Drummond of Hawthornden, scholars at one time thought Ben Jonson had visited Venice and possibly served there as travel guide for Sir Walter Raleigh's son.[34] Now it seems likely that John Florio, the Italian manual writer, dictionary maker, and translator of Montaigne, was the source for Jonson's Venetian information. A copy of *Volpone* autographed to Florio exists, in which Jonson writes to the recipient as 'his loving Father, & worthy Freind, . . . The ayde of his Muses'. Florio also may have contributed some commendatory verse for the volume. In *Volpone*, the dialogue at II,i suggests Jonson's intimate acquaintance with *Second Frutes*. Frances Yates, John Florio's biographer, states conclusively: 'Ben was determined that his Italian comedy *Volpone* should be as painstakingly accurate as his classical plays – not for him vaguely romantic Italy or the Northian Rome of the poet who "wanted art" – and for guidance in his Italian studies he went with his usual thoroughness to the best Italian scholar and teacher of the day, John Florio.'[35]

Volpone presents a more detailed picture of Venice than *The Merchant of Venice* and *Othello* combined. Jonson offers a wealth of local colour, important items of which are absent in Shakespeare though they were popular tourist attractions: the Arsenal (IV,i,91), Grand Canal (V,xii,136), St. Mark's (I,iv,10; IV,vi,67; etc.). Shakespeare can muster gondolas, a courtesan, the Rialto, but Jonson, in addition to these, knows the shops in St. Mark's (I,iv,10) and that Jews loaned money specifically for house furnishings (IV,i,41). His '*Lazaretto*' (IV,i,106) and 'monastery of *San' Spiritio*' (V,xii,131) seem accurate, as are his many Italian words sprinkled throughout the play: '*a sforzato*' (II,ii,45), '*ciarlitani*' (II,ii,49), '*scartoccios*' (II,ii,61), '*canaglia*' (II,ii,71), '*moscadelli*' (II,ii,81), '*unguento*' (II,ii,94), etc. Jonson writes easily of 'Lombard's vinegar' (III,vii,59), 'Bolognian sausages' (V,iv,21), and 'hot Tuscan blood' (III,vii,59). Moryson and many others remarked the mountebanks who 'proclame their wares upon . . . scaffolds', and Jonson's Volpone disguises himself as one such, complete with 'a Zani or Foole'.[36] Moryson adds, 'The people cast their handkerchiefs', and so too does Celia. The biographical details Volpone gives out about Scoto are credible, and the geographical ones are accurate (II,ii).

Sir Politic Wouldbe is easily recognized as a caricature of the contemporary English traveller. He is in Venice 'to observe,/To quote, to learn the language, and so forth' (II,i,12–13). He pretends to know important diplomatic secrets. There must have been many English like Sir Pol, for Florio writes in *Second Frutes* that 'Travellers who boast of a knowledge of foreign affairs are not to be trusted.'[37] Pol's belief in mountebanks ('They are the only knowing men of Europe!' [II,ii,9]), and general wide-eyed innocence while feigning experience makes him wonderfully comic. Lady Pol wants to be up to date; she is in Venice 'for intelligence / Of tires, and fashions, and behavior/Among the courtesans' (II,i,27–9). Peregrine's name suggests his travelling penchant, and what better place to visit than Venice.

But while Jonson's Venetian setting is more specific than Shakespeare's, there are some striking similarities in both playwrights' Venetian plays. Volpone, Mosca, and Iago are all great manipulators of people, talented but villainous play actors and directors who have the ability to produce and perform a scene. Iago's use of Roderigo for his money ('Thus do I ever make my fool my purse' [I,iii,383]) recalls Volpone's plot for gain. When Iago states that he wishes to 'plume up my will' (I,iii,393), one is reminded of Volpone's, 'What should I do/But cocker up my genius' (I,i,70–1). Both Celia and Desdemona are virtuous women in a land famous for courtesans. In Jonson like Shakespeare, men are shown reduced to irrational, animal-like states.

Jonson's inverted fable of men as animals seems almost to take its cue from Gratiano's statement about Shylock in *The Merchant of Venice*, that he holds 'opinion with Pythagoras, / That souls of animals infuse themselves / Into the trunks of men' (IV,i,131–3). Shylock shares with Volpone a gold-centred not God-centred Venice; both have sold their souls. The sequence of Shakespeare's progressive casket scenes echoes Jonson's crescendo of visitors to Volpone's supposed death bed. Both *The Merchant of Venice* and *Volpone* have judicial spectacles full of opportunities for lavish costume displays. In both plays there are courtroom surprises for characters and audiences alike, but in the end appropriate Venetian–English justice is meted out. A masque is planned in *The Merchant of Venice*; one takes place in *Volpone*. Celia and Jessica are both 'kept close', but escape their confinements to affirm their freedom.

The Merchant of Venice may also be compared with *Othello*. Only a part of the action of each play is set in Venice, though the Venetian setting provides an important backdrop for action set elsewhere. Two contrasting worlds are thus presented. Both plays contain independent daughters who, after running away from home, marry against their fathers' wishes. The Jew and the Moor are aliens, 'strangers' to Venice and Venetian manners. Each ultimately confirms his stereotype: Shylock is the sober, vengeful, materialistic Jew who hates Christians, and Othello is characterized as an uncomplicated and primitive Moor who cannot cope in a sophisticated society. The ring Shylock had from his wife Leah smacks of the same magical foreigner stuff that Othello's handkerchief does. Finally, Shylock and Othello are both described as 'old', perhaps hinting in the plays' allegories that primitive Jewish and Moorish cultures predate Christian refinement.

Venice was the hub of Italy for Shakespeare and his contemporaries. One could love it as the locus of excitement and progressive culture, a sort of New York, London, and Paris combined, or hate it as the seat of excess and decadence, a Catholic Sodom and Gomorrah. Most English undoubtedly saw it as a bit of each. Shakespeare's view presents some of the evils and temptations of the place, but also exploits Venice's fascinating appeal. Venice in Shakespeare is, after all, both Portia's and Iago's city.

A THE MERCHANT OF VENICE

Shakespeare inherited the name for Portia's country villa from his *Il Pecorone* source, and he seems more interested in the suggestiveness of the name than Belmont's exact geographical location. Nevertheless, scholars have been tempted to find Belmont on the map. There are some explicit references to its location in the play: it is twenty miles from Venice (III,iv,84), and one can get there by 'traject, . . . the common ferry' (III,iv,53). Though Mario Praz warns 'there are several places named Montabello, so that the impression of a precise place-reference is possibly deceptive', A. Lytton Sells thinks Belmont specifically 'on the hill which overlooks the main road between Vicenza and Verona'.[38] The Euganean Hills west of Padua seems an appropriate setting for Portia's garden estate, since it is an unusually lush and fruitful region. Moreover, the area is associated with poetry: Petrarch died at Arqua in 1374 (traveller Fynes Moryson visited his house and monument).[39] But the mountainous region around Bassano del Grappa has still more appeal as the location of Portia's villa. Though about forty-five, rather than twenty, miles north-west of Venice, it is, nonetheless, near water (the Brenta river and canal), and has impressive estates – like Andrea Palladio's Villa Forcari (1574). The Palazzo Foscarini was visited by Sir Thomas More.[40] This area also has a most suggestive name in terms of Shakespeare's play. The traveller Thomas Coryat knew of 'a certaine Gentleman called Bassano, who . . . lived at a villa that he had in the country'.[41] Another 'Bassano' that many cultured people knew was the painter Jacopo da Ponte, who died in 1592. A number of scholars have remarked Shakespeare's canvaslike Venice in *The Merchant of Venice*, complete with exotic Moor (the Prince of Morocco) and a northern beauty whose 'sunny locks / Hang on her temples like a golden fleece' (I,i,169–70). The name *Bassano* could have suggested Bassanio to Shakespeare.

But aside from references to its location in the play, Belmont seems as much an English country estate as an Italian one. There are other English seeming details as well in *The Merchant of Venice*. Antonio's patronage of Bassanio is consistent with Elizabethan practice, but does not jibe with Moryson's observation that 'In generall all Italians desyre to live of their owne and generously thinck nothing more abject then to depend uppon others for meate or any matenance.'[42] In a Venice of canals, Old Gobbo has a horse named 'Dobbin' (II,ii,95, 96), yet, according to Moryson again, 'The Venetians seldome or never come on horsebacke and vulgar Jeasts are raysed on them for ignorance of ryding.'[43] Coryat writes that he 'saw but one horse in all Venice during the space of sixes weekes that I made my abode there'.[44] Launcelot's mother has the English name 'Margery' (II,ii,89–90), and he worries about his 'rasher on the coals' (III,v,25). The 'rack' on which Portia imagines Bassanio (III,ii,32) is an implement of English torture. The reference to the 'wealthy *Andrew*' (I,i,27) has English not Italian associations. Since the Elizabethans were suspicious of foreigners themselves, it is easy to jump from the Venice of Shakespeare's play to the London of the sixteenth century. Shylock thus becomes, ironically, the proud and alien expatriate Italian (perhaps a language, dancing, fencing teacher, or courtier) perceived as threatening the well-being of native sons.

Shakespeare does attempt, however, to make his Venice a credible Venice. He refers to the expected 'gondilo' (II,viii,8) and surprises with his forementioned accurate *traghetto* detail (III,iv,53).[45] He knows about slaves in Venice (see IV,i,90–3), and the custom of offering pigeons ('a dish of doves') as a gift (II,ii,135). His play has a ruling duke and 'magnificoes' (III,ii,280). More general Italian colour is also evident. Shylock addresses Antonio as 'Signior' (I,iii,106), and Launcelot can slur a word of Italian – '*Fia*' for *Via* (II,ii,11). A 'monast'ry' (III,iv,31) and a masque (II,v,28) are mentioned, as are 'poison' and 'revenge' in Shylock's famous speech (III,i,59–73).

Most of Shakespeare's audience would understand references to the Rialto, and would not have been confused by the prepositions *in*, *on*, or *upon* the playwright used with the noun. They would know that the Rialto was a public place, an area, say, like Wall Street. The sixteenth-century historian William Thomas writes, 'The Rialto is a goodly place in the heart of the city', and Moryson adds that the merchants gather 'at Rialto, where they stand by themselves'.[46] The locus of the area was the exchange itself, which Coryat describes as 'a most stately building . . . where the Venetian Gentlemen and Merchants doe meete twice a day. . . . This Rialto is of a goodly height, built all with bricke as the Palaces are, adorned with many faire walkes or open galleries . . . , and hath a pretty quadrangular court adjoining to it'.[47] Coryat also explains the origin of the word *Rialto*, 'which word is derived from rivue altus, that is a deepe river, because the water is deeper there than about the other islands'.[48] In 1592, just before Shakespeare wrote *The Merchant of Venice*, Antonio da Ponte completed the renowned Rialto Bridge, a structure that was very much on the tongues of English travellers returning from Venice. Coryat labels it 'the fairest bridge by many degrees for one arch that ever I saw'.[49] Moryson reports that the Venetians consider it the 'eighth miracle of the world'.[50]

In the *Il Pecorone* source, the disguised wife-lawyer comes from Bologna, a city famous for its law school.[51] Padua was more renowned for the training of physicians, but its general reputation as an educational centre perhaps prompted Shakespeare to use it instead of Bologna for his play. The name of Portia's cousin, Bellario, is, surprisingly, a correct Paduan one.[52] Genoa was reputed a city for usury, and as a place 'where women have . . . much liberty'.[53] It was a cosmopolitan seaport; hence, Jessica might credibly spend 'fourscore ducats' there in 'one night' (III,i,109).

Shakespeare was probably familiar with actual Italian merchant ships like Antonio's, because they docked regularly along the estuary of the Thames in London. Moryson describes them as 'From five hundreth to twelve hundreth Tonne, . . . being built large in the Wast and Keele for Capacitye of Merchandize.'[54] Moryson further notes that these 'Shipps are heavy in sayling and great of burthen and the Governors' & Mariners not very expert, nor bold.'[55] There was a Venetian law on the books that merchant ships of five hundred tons or more had to carry both native youth and two 'other' boys to 'breede them Mariners'.[56] By the end of the sixteenth century, one might infer from the concern with maritime skill, too many Venetians must have heeded the old Italian proverb quoted by Moryson: *'Leda il lar', sta su la terra'* [Praise the sea-tide, on land abide].[57] Moryson observes that 'the old Conquerors of the World, are at this day so effiminate and so inamoured of their Paradise of Italy, as nothing but desperate fortune can make them undertake any voyages by Sea, or Land'.[58]

Thus, while Venetian ships, according to the English traveller George Sandys, might 'fly abroad in exceeding abundance to all places, and in wealth (wherever they come) overtop all other',[59] merchants like Shakespeare's Antonio tended to stay at home. Such wealthy merchants were the backbone of the economic system of many Italian cities. Merchant financiers loaned money to governments and rulers at very high rates of interest, but they were not labelled usurers.[60] Only the smaller financier was regulated, his license granted by the municipal council. This so-called 'usurer' loaned relatively small amounts of money to all comers. Merchant financiers and public usurers were never confused.

As a seaport and centre for trade, the 'market place of the world' in Coryat's phrase,[61] it was only good business for Venice to be tolerant of foreigners and provide freedoms for a heterogeneous population. During his visit to Venice, Coryat observed 'Polonians, Slavonians, Persians, Grecians, Turks, Jewes, Christians of all the famousest regions of all Christendome': 'Here you may both see all manner of fashions of attire, and heare all the languages of Christendome, besides those that are spoken by the barbarous Ethnickes . . .'.[62] There was comparative religious tolerance in Venice. Thomas remarks somewhat excessively: 'If thou be a Jew, a Turk, or believest in the devil (so thou spread not thine opinions abroad), thou art free from all controlment.'[63] Roger Ascham linked 'Jewish, Turkish, Papish, and Devilish' all in a group when speaking of Venetian religious freedom.[64]

The Jewish 'freedom' in Venice was closely circumscribed. Jews were required to live in a 'ghetto', the first of its kind, and the one which has given us the English word. The site of this Jewish enclave from the early sixteenth century was an abandoned foundry (the old Venetian dialect word *geto* means 'foundry'). Moryson describes the area: 'each family hath a little house, and all have one court-yard common, so as they live as it were in a Colledge, or almes-house'.[65] Coryat adds that the ghetto 'is enclosed round about with water', and contains 'in all betwixt five and six thousand' persons.[66] Jews had to wear identifying badges. Moryson observes a typical 'Redd or Yellowe Capp, or more commonly a little bonett or hatt.'[67] (Though there was undoubtedly some easily recognizable Jewish dress in the Elizabethan theatre, there seems to be no historical 'Jewish gaberdine' [I,iii,112] as in Shakespeare's play.) Venetian Jews were 'not allowed to buy any lands, howses or [have] stable inheritances'.[68] Moryson's remark that 'the Jewes live in no respect no not the most learned or richest of them' is especially interesting when one remembers the high social place of many Venetian courtesans.[69] Moryson's comments about Jews are coloured by undisguised contemporary prejudice. For Moryson the Jewish people 'are a miserable nation', and he has difficulty understanding Italian princes who allow 'Jewes into their Cittyes, and permitt them to use horrible extortion upon their subjectes, in the lending of mony.'[70] He reports a normal interest rate of 'five in the hundreth', but the usurers 'may take as they can agree'.[71] Shylock's hatred for Antonio is partly because 'He lends out money gratis, and brings down/The rate of usance' (I,iii,44–5); Shakespeare's Jew is proud of his 'bargains' and his 'well-won thrift' (I,iii,50). Thomas observes that because of the high interest rate, 'the Jews are out of measure wealthy'.[72]

Shylock's Jewish world in *The Merchant of Venice* is pictured by Shakespeare as austere, sober, and insulated. The shutters are closed against masques and music. And Lorenzo warns, 'The man that hath no music in himself, . . . / Is fit for treasons, stratagems, and spoils; / . . . Let no such man be trusted' (V,i,83–8). Shylock apparently starves his servant Launcelot, and repeatedly refuses social communion with his Christian clients who bid him 'dine with us' (I,iii,32). Predictably he objects to 'feasting forth' (II,v,37), 'to smell pork, to eat of the habitation which your prophet the Nazarite conjur'd the devil into' (I,iii,33–5). But at last, after dreaming of 'moneybags', the Jew agrees to 'go in hate, to feed upon/The prodigal Christian' (II,v,14–15). It is as if he will eat with them to 'spend' their food. Shylock's Jewish teaching is subject to twisted reading of authority, as in the Jacob and the ewes exegesis. While Shakespeare's usurer seems to love his daughter, he imprisons her in his lifeless world, a world which she describes as 'hell' (II,iii,2). Shylock's language is mostly prosaic, halting, repetitive; his one eloquent appeal for his humanity allows him hope for resurrection from his dead life through conversion.

Marlowe's Jewish merchant of Malta, Barabas, is converted by Shakespeare into a Christian merchant of Venice, Antonio. If Marlowe's merchant engenders all the clichés of Jewish and Machiavellian selfish greed, Shakespeare's embodies just the opposite. In his play, Shakespeare is saying that being a merchant is not the bad thing; being a Jew is. The Renaissance English were merchants too, and proud of their entrepreneurial prowess. It is the usurer Shylock who assumes many of Barabas' negative traits – hate for Christians, the will to revenge, etc. Both Barabas and Shylock feel licensed to deceive Christians. As Jews they feel the 'law' is their ally. Shylock says, 'I crave the law' (IV,i,206) and Barabas, too, exclaims, 'Let me have law' (V,i,39). Jessica and Abigail are similar daughters, beautiful women who ultimately see the light and convert to Christianity.[73] Unlike Barabas, however, Shylock does not 'count religion but a childish toy' (Pro. l.14).

The settings in *The Merchant of Venice* reflect two worlds. Venice and Belmont suggest the schizophrenic love/hate relationship Renaissance England had with Italy. For if the 'Venetian' side of Italy was perceived as fallen, one of false religion and immorality (courtesans, Machiavelli, the Pope), the 'Belmont' side conjured up music, classics, the poetry of Petrarch, the gentility of Castiglione – in a word, humanistic learning and culture.

The contrasting settings of Venice and Belmont can be viewed further as representing not Italy at all, but rather a newer and older England. Commercial Venice thus would be the commercial London of the late sixteenth century, a thriving port metropolis. The merchant venturer is king here; fortunes are made and lost by courageous individual risk-takers, and even foreigners might be rich. Social and economic mobility is possible. Belmont, on the other hand, would recall an older England – the estates of the landed aristocracy with family wealth and name. A child is responsible to her father's will; the feudal notion of contentment with 'place' obtains. If one was born, say, a shoemaker, since God ordained this in his perfectly created scheme of things, one should not aspire to some other trade or vocation.

There is still another possible interpretation for the double setting in *The Merchant of Venice*. Belmont could be England, and Venice could be Italy. Shakespeare's play portrays Venice as a masculine world ruled by a Duke, where even women dress as men to pursue their 'business'; it is a public world of 'work'. Conversely, Belmont is feminine, private, and homey; suitors from other lands come to it with marriage hopes. Like the real Pope for Venice, the foreigner Shylock is a presence in Shakespeare's city, and what breeds here is money, hatred, and false religion. Like Shakespeare's queen in England, the native Portia is mistress in Belmont, and she will have no alien to wed. Nature and music, love and poetry are found in Belmont; a harsh Jew, cruel bond, court of law, even a cancelled masque, are discovered in Venice.

In the play's mythology, of course, the contrasting worlds are not specifically place oriented at all really, but rather emphatically Jewish and Christian. Launcelot Gobbo's monologue as he is about to move from the Jew Shylock to the Christian Bassanio is more than a comic touch. Launcelot imagines himself in a Faustian situation, with supposedly good angels at one elbow reminding him of his 'duty' to fulfil his servile bond, and supposedly bad angels at the other exhorting him to follow his inner impulses and leave the Jew (II,ii,1–32). Launcelot eventually decides to take the Christian's livery, and thus converts his 'famish'd service' (II,ii,106). While Shylock is 'the devil incarnation' (II,ii,27–8), he describes his new master Bassanio as having 'the grace of God' (II,ii,150–1).

Launcelot's observations serve as a backdrop to Antonio's action. The merchant has pledged his body only and not his soul to the devil as in the Faust legend. He will be saved not condemned when his bond comes due because he has agreed to its condition as an expression of generous love and friendship, not for selfish personal gain as in Faust's case. Like Bassanio when selecting from among the caskets, Antonio makes a Christian choice – he hazards all for the right reasons. The merchant knows that 'the world [is] but . . . the world' (I,i,77), and that his true 'estate' is not wholly tied to it. When his bond expires he is 'saved' by Portia, a Christ-like virgin of mercy who shows herself adhering to her father's 'law' but adding her own kind of humanizing spirit to his letter. Antonio lends money for 'Christian cur'sy' (III,i,49), and displays the virtue of Christian 'patience' (IV,i,11) and a readiness to pay 'with all . . . heart' (IV,i,281). If the garden of Belmont is not his reward as it is Bassanio's, a more heavenly beautiful mountain, a 'City of God', is implied just inheritance for his generosity. For the moment at the end of the play, however, he must remain in the mercantile hell of Venice, the 'City of Man'.

There are three Christian everymen in *The Merchant of Venice*, fished for variously by Shylock, the representative of false religion. Gobbo is a simple and comic everyman who yet can see the hunger and bondage of service to Judaism. His Christian name has both English and ironic associations, as we recall King Arthur's heroic follower. Bassanio's name suggests 'touchstone' (from *basanite*), the stone used to test for true gold. Bassanio, almost like Spenser's Red Cross Knight, seems the representative Protestant Englishman who makes an appropriate marriage not only to his love, but by allegorical extension to his Queen and true church. Antonio's name recalls saints, and he is the special Christian singled out by God for a higher calling – to denounce false religion and be a willing martyr for the values of the true faith. The devil Shylock is defeated in one way or another by each of these Christian everymen.

The Merchant of Venice is partly and importantly a play about conversion. After agreeing to Shylock's bond, Antonio punningly exclaims: 'Hie thee, gentle Jew', then explains, 'The Hebrew will turn Christian, he grows kind' (I,iii,177–8). Portia is explicit about her love for Bassanio: 'Myself, and what is mine, to you and yours / Is now converted' (III,ii,166–7). Portia, Nerissa, and Jessica all are converted by love, and disguise themselves to follow their men. Jessica says: 'I shall be sav'd by my husband, he hath made me a Christian!' (III,v,19–20). Shylock, too, must 'become a Christian' (IV,i,387), despite his plea that 'You take my house when you do take the prop / That doth sustain my house' (IV,i,375–6). And Launcelot Gobbo, to be sure, worries about the effect that the conversions will have on the price of pork (III,v,21–6)!

The alien house of Jewish lead, representing by extension and transference the foreign and sordid Italy of the Pope's false religion, must be converted to English Protestant 'gold' in the play's alchemy. With the help of friendship and love, the representative Englishman Bassanio translates genteel poverty and a leaden casket into a golden future. Angels in Belmont's true Christian world are to sing not spend, the stars above are 'bright gold' (V,i,59–61). Everything is in its rightful place. Shylock's wealth is seen as fool's gold, death dealing. Ironically, the Jew's insistence upon his bond does him in: the law alone, without tempering mercy, leads to defeat and damnation. The Jew, like the Pope in Shakespeare's allegory, is committed to the riches of this world (a common Protestant charge), and the eventual end of this world is death not salvation.

Judaism is, to be sure, associated with Old Testament law. Venice, too, had a renowned legal system. Venetian law and justice was famous throughout Renaissance Europe, and Shakespeare exploits this reputation in *The Merchant of Venice*. Moryson observes that 'The Italyans in generall are most strict in the courses of Justice.'[74] He notes, 'The Civill laweyers must study 8 yeares, and the Cannonists 5 yeares, before they be made Doctours, and they must be examined privately and publikely.'[75] To Moryson, it is the Italian tradition of working with two sets of law that accounts for the development of fine legal minds: 'Italy being most governed by the Imperiall and Papall lawes and both much swaying in all Christian

Kingdomes, the Italyans for the great rewarde thereof much following those Studyes, their Universities have yealded and still Yealde many famous men for the knowledge of these lawes.'[76] Says Thomas, 'this is clear: there can be no better order of justice in a commonwealth than theirs'.[77] The *Il Pecorone* source claims Venice as not only 'a place where the law was enforced', but even where 'the law has become too strict'.[78]

Shakespeare suggests that Jewish law is limited, and Venetian law is just. But the English not the Venetian system is clearly at work in *The Merchant of Venice*. A monarch answerable to God is superior to a republican order answerable, it was thought by the English, to a Pope and his Inquisition. Like Portia, the Queen can intrude into the system, meting out the true justice not possible with the power-limited Duke.

Shakespeare apparently knew little about the place of the Doge in the judicial system of his city.[79] The Doge, for example, did not preside over the Venetian court; neither did magnificoes act as judges. The playwright writes a memorable trial scene, perhaps the premier judicial spectacle in literature, but his dramatic rightness is factually wrong. The references are to imagined not actual Venetian practices.

Shylock challenges the Duke with his bond: 'If you deny it, let the danger light / Upon your charter and your city's freedom!' (IV,i,38–9). He adds, 'If you deny me, fie upon your law! / There is no force in the decrees of Venice' (IV,i,101–2). Antonio has pointed out earlier that as a trading centre Venice had to be especially careful with its justice:

> The duke cannot deny the course of law;
> For the commodity that strangers have
> With us in Venice, if it be denied,
> Will much impeach the justice of the state,
> Since that the trade and profit of the city
> Consisteth of all nations.
>
> (III,iii,26–31)

Neither can the Duke capriciously change the law to fit a particular circumstance; Portia notes, "Twill be recorded for a precedent' (IV,i,220). Since Shakespeare's Venetian court is dramatic and not real, he can heighten his effect at will, as for instance when he invents a law concerning death and confiscation of goods as punishment for plots against a Venetian citizen:

> It is enacted in the laws of Venice,
> If it be proved against an alien,
> That by direct or indirect attempts
> He seek the life of any citizen,
> The party 'gainst the which he doth contrive
> Shall seize one half his goods; the other half
> Comes to the privy coffer of the state,
> And the offender's life lies in the mercy
> Of the Duke only, 'gainst all other voice.
>
> (IV,i,348–56)[80]

Shakespeare, thus, takes on the most respected and famous system of law in Renaissance Europe, and devalues it at the expense of English law. English law is the play's benevolent 'Venetian' law, interpreted by a merciful monarch-like Portia and presided over by a Duke. Allegorically, in turn, 'real' Venetian law becomes Catholic–Jewish law interpreted by a Pope-like Shylock.

The two legal systems at odds generalize to two opposing visions of man's destiny: the Christian (that is, Protestant) and the Jewish (that is, Catholic). The Protestant–Christian promises mercy and salvation, while the Catholic–Jewish means death. The symbol of conversion to the Jewish side is circumcision. The symbol of Christian choice for salvation is to be found in the absent father's lottery of the three caskets. The tragic and comic plots of the play can be seen as necessary for one another, tying the play together.

Circumcision, the 'bond' of the covenant, is a central ritual of Jewish faith. The Jew–devil–Pope Shylock would convert the true Protestant–Christian–Englishman Antonio by way of a sinister bond. Afterwards, he would 'bait fish withal' (III,i,53), catch other Christian–Englishmen with his pound of Antonio's flesh. If Christ would fish to save, Shylock would fish to destroy. In a possible source for *The Merchant of Venice*, Declamation 95 of *The Orator* (1596), the Jew here considers cutting off the Christian's 'privie members, supposing that the same would altogether weigh a just pound'.[81] Circumcision by extension becomes castration, as in Shakespeare's play it is generalized to include excising the true Christian's life-blood. The merchant's conversion would be ritualized by a pound of flesh circumcised from near the 'heart' (IV,i,233), the symbolic seat of Christian generosity, love, music, gentility. The Italian–Catholic–Jew, that is, wishes to cut out the essential English Christian spirit. The 'unfortunate traveller' Jack Wilton, in Thomas Nashe's romance, describes how he was taken prisoner by a 'foreskin clipper', then sold to another Jew for his 'yearly anatomy'. Jack notes wryly, 'theres no such readie way to make a man a true Christian, as to perswade himselfe he is taken up for anatomie'.[82] To Elizabethan Christians, circumcision suggested life-denying mutilation. But they were fascinated with it. Coryat reveals his disappointment at not being able to witness a circumcision when in Italy.[83] Enemy infidels, too, as well as Jews were circumcised monsters. Marlowe's Barabas is conspiratorial with his slave Ithamore: 'we are villains both!/– Both circumcised' (II,ii,220–1), unlike the 'swine-eating Christians –/Unchosen nation, never circumcis'd' (II,iii,7–8). At the climactic end to his play, the murderer Othello calls himself 'circumcised dog' (V,ii,355).

If the bond to Judaism and what it represents allegorically in Venice is life-denying, the caskets in Belmont are life-affirming, containing a Christian message. The leaden casket holds the golden world of love, salvation, mercy, and marriage. It is the hopeful future not the fallen past. Portia's presumably Muslim Morroco cannot choose correctly; neither can Spain's presumably Catholic Arragon. The absent father God sets up a lottery of spirit for the virgin queen. With her marriage to the symbol for the true Protestant Englishman, she can put fallen Venice behind and claim a new Eden. The bickering about the rings at the end of the play perhaps suggests that this new world is not to be construed as completely Edenic, however. It is still earthly, with human playfulness and imperfection.

For Roger Ascham and others, conversion to a false religion or even atheism was a clear and present danger for young English travellers in Venice. Although there were Jews and infidels in this swarming port city, temptation was thought to lie mostly with the native Catholic population because of their perceived sophistication and worldliness. With some adept dramatic transference, Shakespeare makes his Venetians not Catholics explicitly but Christians generally, his bogeyman not specifically the Pope but the Jew. The Jew would convert the Christian rather than the Italian Catholic the English Protestant. At the same time, Shakespeare exploits the more general popular appeal of Venice as a setting, invoking its foreign attractiveness and sea-oriented familiarity for the English. And he presents as a retreat the fairy-tale Belmont, a world of the comfortable past and the hopeful future.

B OTHELLO

Like *The Merchant of Venice*, *Othello* has two different settings. Only Act I of the tragedy is located in Venice; the rest of the play takes place on a 'warlike isle' (II,iii,57), the outpost of Cyprus in the eastern Mediterranean. Until 1570 Cyprus was under Venetian control, a frontier of sorts for Christian Europe against the Turks. Though a full 1300 nautical miles from Venice (and only 750 from Constantinople), it represented a strategic fortress in the face of a perpetual Ottoman threat. It was also perceived by some as a possible launching point for a new Christian Crusade to recapture the East. By 1 August 1571, however, Cyprus was lost. The Ottoman Empire had established itself as the primary military power in the region. At the turn of the century Moryson writes that Venice paid 'yearely tribute' to the Turks, despite the fact that they 'seemed of purpose to provoke the Venetians with continuall injuries'.[84]

The Turkish seige of Famagusta, from 18 September 1570 until 1 August 1571, is in the sketchy historical background of *Othello*. The chief port city of Cyprus, Famagusta was the seat of the Venetian governors during the fifteenth and sixteenth centuries. In the spring of 1570 the Ottomans invaded Cyprus, and the Venetians concentrated their forces at two strategic places, the island's capital of Nicosia and at Famagusta. Nicosia was attacked first, and fell to the Turks by August of 1570. In the words of one modern historian, the aftermath was horrible: 'The usually well-disciplined Janissaries streamed into the city and went berserk, looting or destroying everything within sight and killing every single person they found still alive.'[85] Even while Nicosia was falling, defensive lines were strengthened around Famagusta on land, and at sea something of a small fleet was on alert in the harbour. Supplies were brought in from Candia on Crete. The Turkish general, Mustafa Pasha, however, had an estimated 120 000 troops. For a short time, though, luck was on the Venetian side. Before Mustafa could complete his trenches and bring up his cannons, 'the Turkish admiral Pirali Pasha sent word that he feared for the safety of his fleet because the bad autumn gales were expected shortly . . .'.[86] Thus, just as in Shakespeare's play, the Venetians are saved for the moment because of the weather. But in history, only for a short time. Autumn over, the seige began in earnest. After a prolonged and heroic defense, and following nearly a year of holding out against overwhelming odds, the noble Venetians surrendered their city. The cruelty of the Turks to the Venetian commanders, following promises of safe-conduct, sent shock waves throughout the entire European Christian community and, some suggest, led ultimately to the Holy League alliance that resulted in the Battle of Lepanto. In any case, Astor Baglione, the General-in-Chief of the army of Cyprus, was slaughtered in front of his enemy, the Turkish commander. Marc Antonio Bragadino, captain of the town, endured an even worse fate. His nose and ears were first cut off, then he was paraded before the Turkish batteries on hands and knees bearing dirt and forced to kiss the ground, next he was exposed in the market place, and, finally, he was flayed alive before Mustafa Pasha.[87] This sadistic barbarity associated with the historical Cyprus of the late sixteenth century gives a kind of suggestive backdrop to Iago's excessive and horrifying behaviour in Shakespeare's play.

In *Othello*, Cyprus still belongs to Venice, perhaps only because of the fortunate tempest at sea. The action takes place in 'a town of war, / Yet wild' (II,iii,213-14); the population consists mostly of soldiers and their followers. Just beneath the surface order of the island, chaos and anarchy are potential. Here government can be subverted by some of those pledged to maintain it; men can act as beasts, the marriage bed can become a death bed. The outpost of Cyprus is drawn as the antithesis of civilized Venice.

Unlike the garden retreat of Belmont in *The Merchant of Venice*, Cyprus in *Othello* contrasts negatively with Venice. The Venice of the tragedy is also a more sympathetic place than the Venice of the comedy. 'My lord,' exclaims Lodovico when Othello strikes Desdemona on Cyprus, 'this would not be believ'd in Venice' (IV,i,242). Venice is presented as a place of gentility, refinement, sophistication, practised government. When Brabantio is aroused at night by Roderigo and Iago, he is incredulous: 'This is Venice; / My house is not a grange' (I,i,104–6). Such behaviour as thievery or abduction is inconceivable in his civilized city.

As in *The Merchant of Venice*, Shakespeare includes some Venetian and more general Italian detail in *Othello*. He alludes to a 'gundolier'

(I,i,125), 'mountebanks' (I,iii,61), magnificoes, signoirs, and an Inn named the 'Sagittary' (I,i,158; I,iii,115).[88] The play contains a courtesan and is centrally about jealousy, proverbial with Italians. Words like 'revenge' (III,iii,459) and 'poison' (I,iii,112; III,iii,325, 326, 389, etc.) spice the dialogue. Surprising because the details are so specific, Shakespeare mentions the Venetian 'officers of night' (I,i,182), and knows that a Tuscan like Cassio might credibly refer to 'a twiggen bottle' (II,iii,148), the kind that holds Chianti. But 'small beer' (II,i,160) and an 'alehouse' (II,i,139) are also mentioned, and the songs seem English. What is most remarkable in a play about Venice and war, however, is that no mention is made of the city's famous Arsenal. Thomas, for example, was so impressed with it that he found it Venice's most notable building, even exceeding the Church of St. Mark: 'For there they have well near 200 galleys in such an order that upon a very small warning they may be furnished out unto the sea.'[89] Thomas further remarks the enormous supply storage facilities for the raw material to maintain and build ships and weapons. Tourists Moryson and Coryat, too, were very impressed with Venice's Arsenal.[90]

Shakespeare received his information about a Moor as the Venetian general from his Cinthio source, but the detail is historically credible as well. Thomas writes of the Venetian practice of engaging foreigners for command posts in order to prevent *coups d'état* by popular leaders and thus subvert the republican system of government: 'they are served of strangers, both for general, for captains, and for all other men of war, because their law permitteth not any Venetian to be captain over an army by land, fearing, I think, Caesar's example'.[91] Perhaps one reason for promoting Cassio instead of Iago is because he is a Florentine and not a native Venetian, though this is not mentioned in the play. Thomas' assessment that Venetians were not expert 'men of war' seems confirmed in *Othello*: the Venetians win against the Turks by sheer luck, their intelligence reports about their enemy's movements and strength are faulty, and the Duke seems characterized a jingling, self-satisfied ruler, certainly not a leader and military strategist.

Cinthio stereotypes Moors as 'so hot by nature that any little thing moves . . . [them] to anger and revenge'.[92] This description of Moors also represents precisely one aspect of the English stereotype of the Italian. Quick to assume a wrong, it was thought by Moryson and others, 'he is very likely to take revenge and that very deepe beyond the quality of the offence'.[93] One of Nashe's villains exclaims: 'All true Italians imitate me in revenging constantly . . .'.[94]

Though Moor, Othello is not an Italian in Shakespeare's play; indeed, in some ways he is very insecure in his Venetian setting. For one thing, Othello is self-conscious about his 'Rude . . . speech' (I,iii,81). He explains, 'I am black, / And have not those soft parts of conversation / That chamberers have' (III,iii,263–5). When he greets his wife after he has landed on Cyprus, he fears his public outburst has been excessive: 'I prattle out of fashion' (II,i,206). Age, too, is a factor in his discomfort (see III,iii,265–6). Othello relies on Iago, therefore, who claims to know 'our country disposition well' (III,iii,201). The general trusts his ensign to interpret Venetian customs and manners for him, as for example when he presses Iago to tell him what is going on between Desdemona and Cassio. Ultimately, the Moor seems to confirm for himself what he has feared all along: an aging black and unsophisticated soldier is not an appropriate match for a young and white 'super-subtle Venetian' (I,iii,356). Othello seems a bit like Cyprus: for the moment he has a clothing of civilization over his rough essence, but waiting to erupt at any moment are dark forces – primitive and elemental chaos. Like Cyprus, Othello is contested territory; he is presumably a comparatively newly-minted Christian married to good Desdemona, but seduced by his Ottoman self and the devilish Iago. 'Are we turn'd Turks' (II,iii,170), he can say, emphasizing the Venetian–Christian values of civility and government in the face of barbaric behaviour. But his own forces of darkness overcome his better self, so that, finally, he must take 'by th' throat the circumcised dog' (V,ii,355–6), his evil self, and kill it.

Brabantio is a pillar of Venetian society, a senator and a father. He cannot understand why Desdemona, 'in spite of nature, / Of years, of country, credit, every thing' (I,iii,96–7), has eloped with Othello, rejecting 'The wealthy curled darlings of our nation' (I,ii,68). Venetian women were supposed to marry to further their families' social, economic, and political position. Thomas quotes a father on the subject: 'If I spend largely with my daughter, it is because I will bestow her on a gentleman Venetian to increase the nobility of mine own blood and by means of such alliance, to attain more ability to rule and reign in my commonwealth.'[95] Moryson writes of the usual marriage arrangement: 'They marrye upon agreement of Parents without having seene one another, and the husband takes a noble wife only with purpose to have Children by her little caring that her person may content him, since he is free with strange women to satisfy his desyres.'⁹⁶ Only courtesans had some freedom to choose their men. It is no wonder then that Brabantio is upset at his daughter's marriage. The Duke, too, sympathizes before he knows the facts, and in a dramatically contrived breach of fabled Venetian justice he promises Brabantio, 'the bloody book of law/You shall yourself read in the bitter letter/ After your own sense; yea, though our proper son / Stood in your action' (I,iii,67–70). In Venetian law, a wronged party, even a senator, did not sentence an offender. The Duke's pardon of his General after only an informal hearing also falls outside actual Venetian practice.⁹⁷

At times scholars have questioned whether Michael Cassio is Veronese or Florentine, but the overwhelming consensus is that the word 'Veronesa' ('Veronessa' in Qq; 'Verennessa' in the Folio) refers to 'The ship . . . here put in' (II,i,25) and not the gentleman.⁹⁸ Primarily because of Machiavelli, Florence was associated in the English mind with warfare; thus, Shakespeare's soldier comes from an appropriate place. Cassio's training seems to have been of the reserve officer type. According to Iago, Cassio is a theorist rather than a practiced soldier. As a banking and economic centre, Florence had a reputation for mathematical expertise, and when Iago calls Cassio 'a great arithmetician' and 'this counter-caster' (I,i,19, 31) he is perhaps slurring what he perceives as the new breed of theorist, strategist, and technician.⁹⁹ Also by way of Machiavelli, Florence was thought of as a school for politicians. Iago accuses Cassio of pulling strings to secure his lieutenant's rank (I,i,36–7) – most ironic coming from a person who employed 'Three great ones of the city' (I,i,8) on his own behalf. Despite his native roots, however, Cassio is not a good politician. His approaches to Desdemona are not his own idea, and they are not very well handled.

Cassio also evidences more generally perceived Italian traits. Iago characterizes him as 'rash and very sudden in choler' (II,i,272), and his inability to hold his drink makes for behaviour 'full of quarrel' (II,iii,50). The Florentine's 'very poor and unhappy brains for drinking' (II,iii,33–4), in addition to a necessary plot device, perhaps is Shakespeare's way of redirecting charges of English intemperance by expatriate Italians such as John Florio, who flaunted supposed Italian sobriety in England.¹⁰⁰ We recall the villain Iago's slur against the English in this regard (II, iii,76–85). Cassio, like Othello, is also an innocent in some ways. He believes Iago to be 'kind and honest' as any Florentine (III,i,40). Finally, Cassio's treatment of Bianca and talk about her seems cavalier – he is obviously more concerned with his own reputation than with hers.

But despite his faults, Cassio comes across in the play as primarily a gentleman, more in accord with the positive side of Florence's reputation. Moryson writes that 'the Florentines are reputed Courteous, modest, grave, wise, and excellent in many vertues'.[101] Cassio refuses to respond in kind to Iago's suggestive comments about Desdemona (see II,iii,13–29). When the soldiers discuss salvation, the Florentine affirms that he hopes to be saved, but adds 'no offence to the general, nor any man of quality' (II,iii,106–7). Cassio seems without excessive ambition; when Othello's boat has not yet come in to shore, he 'looks sadly, / And prays the Moor be safe' (II,i,32–3), though presumably he would be next in line to succeed the general. After greeting Emilia with a kiss (II,i,99), Cassio excuses his good 'manners' to Iago as 'breeding', and 'courtesy' (II,i,98–9). Following this incident, Iago sneers in an aside at the socially apt lieutenant attending Desdemona:

> He takes her by the palm; ay, well said, whisper. With as little a web as this will I ensnare as great a fly as Cassio. Ay, smile upon her, do; I will gyve thee in thine own courtship. You say true, 'tis so indeed. If such tricks as these strip you out of your lieutenantry, it had been better you had not kiss'd your three fingers so oft, which now again you are most apt to play the sir in. Very good; well kiss'd! an excellent courtesy! 'Tis so indeed. Yet again, your fingers to your lips? Would they were clysterpipes for your sake! . . .
>
> (II,i,167–77)

Florence must have been reputed for hand kissing, for Barabas, in Marlowe's *The Jew of Malta*, reports that he 'learn'd in Florence how to kiss my hand' (II,iii,23).

The purest dialect of Italian was thought to be spoken in Tuscany, and the Florentines were reported 'great talkers', accompanying their speech with arm waving: 'For he is not reputed a man among them that cannot play the orator in his tale, as well as in gesture as in word.'[102] Cassio's eloquence is one of his distinguishing features in the play. He can turn a phrase: Othello's 'bark is stoutly timber'd, and his pilot / Of very expert and approv'd allowance; / Therefore my hopes (not surfeited to death) / Stand in bold cure' (II,i,48–51).

When the Florentine describes Desdemona, he rhapsodizes: she 'paragons description and wild fame;/[she is] One that excels the quirks of blazoning pens, / And in th' essential vesture of creation / Does tire the ingener' (II,i,62–5). These lines begin what amounts to a lyrical epithalamion. Cassio greets Desdemona on shore as a goddess: 'let her have your knees. / Hail to thee, lady! and the grace of heaven, / Before, behind thee, and on every hand, / Enwheel her round!' (II,i,84–7). His poetic gallantry in speaking to Desdemona is ongoing: 'Bounteous madam, / What ever shall become of Michael Cassio, / He's never any thing but your true servant' (III,iii,7–9); or,

> . . . I do beseech you
> That by your virtuous means I may again
> Exist, and be a member of his love
> Whom I, with all the office of my heart,
> Entirely honor. I would not be delay'd.
> If my offence be of such mortal kind
> That nor my service past, nor present sorrows,
> Nor purpos'd merit in futurity,
> Can ransom me into his love again,
> But to know so much be my benefit;
> So shall I clothe me in a forc'd content,
> And shut myself up in some other course
> To fortune's alms.
>
> (III,iv,110–22)

Shakespeare's Iago is a devilish Machiavellian, but his prototype in Giraldi Cinthio's *Hecatommithi* (seventh novella, third decade) is even worse. Cinthio's villain derives from Senecan models, and could be Spanish in origin.[103] Shakespeare gives Iago a Spanish name, but makes his nationality apparently Venetian. It is as if he compounds the negative in his Iago – that is, he combines the hostile suggestion of England's Catholic enemy with the suggestion of the seamy Italian. Iago's native citizenship emphasizes Othello's foreignness and dependence. The general relies on his ensign to be conversant with Venetian ways, especially as they relate to women. He believes Iago completely when he says of wives: 'In Venice they do let God see the pranks / They dare not show their husbands; their best conscience / Is not to leave't undone, but keep't unknown' (III,iii,202–4). To Iago all women are adultresses, whores, 'fitchews'.

There is a spectrum of women in *Othello* representing three distinct types, and Iago does not relate well to any of them. Emilia is the pragmatic spouse who would do anything 'for all the world' (IV,iii,68), Bianca is the courtesan, and Desdemona the chaste and loyal wife.

Something is obviously wrong with Iago's marriage. Emilia knows about husbands who lose interest: 'I do think it is . . . husbands' faults/If wives do fall; . . . they slack their duties,/And pour our treasures into foreign laps' (IV,iii,86–8). She explains: '"Tis not a year or two shows us a man:/They are all but stomachs, and we all but food;/They eat us hungerly, and when they are full/They belch us' (III,iv,103–6). Emilia seems especially anxious to please her husband; thus, he can use her to prod Desdemona about Cassio's suit (II,iii,383–4) and to get the handkerchief: 'My *wayward* husband hath a hundred times/Woo'd me to steal it' (III,iii,292–3; italics mine). In the Cinthio source, Iago and Emilia have a young child who diverts Desdemona while Iago takes the handkerchief, but in Shakespeare's play the couple is childless.[104] Emilia works hard at her marriage; in the end, however, Iago still considers his wife a 'Villainous whore' (V,ii,229). In his mind she has cuckolded him with both Othello and Cassio: 'I do suspect the lusty Moor/Hath leap'd into my seat; . . . [and] I fear Cassio with my night-cap too' (II,i,295–6, 307). Emilia's suspected adultery is uppermost in Iago's stated motivation for revenge: 'I hate the Moor,/And it is thought abroad that 'twixt my sheets/H'as done my office' (I,iii,386–8). At one point in the play, Iago catches Cassio and Emilia in a rather compromising position. The lieutenant has just asked the Clown to call forth Emilia as Iago enters. To cover his guilty appearance of asking for Iago's wife when she is alone at home, Cassio explains: 'I have made bold, Iago,/To send in to your wife' (III,i,33–4), and then he adds, obviously self-conscious, 'My suit to her/Is that she will to virtuous Desdemona/Procure me some access' (III,i,34–6). Surely Iago does not believe this man who he has himself described as 'fram'd to make women false' (I,iii,398). Emilia shows that she is familiar with a jealous husband and his irrationality in her conversation with Desdemona (III,iv,159–62). Ultimately, of course, Iago reveals his hatred for his wife and kills her.

In effect Iago also kills Desdemona – he even suggests the method to Othello: 'Do it not with poison; strangle her in her bed, even the bed she hath contaminated' (IV,i,207–8). Iago claims to love

Desdemona, but his love is perverse. He feels not 'absolute lust' for her; rather, he wishes to use her for his 'revenge' (II,i,291–4). No woman is honest in his opinion. He tells Roderigo that Desdemona cannot love the Moor for very long: 'when she is sated with his body, she will find the error of her choice. She must have change, she must' (I,iii,350–2). She will next fall for Cassio (II,i,221–48, 287). Iago's off-colour remarks about Desdemona to Cassio – that she is 'sport for Jove', 'full of game', with an inviting eye and a come-on voice (II,iii,17–27) – indicate that he thinks of her mostly in animalistic terms, a 'white ewe' hungry for a 'black ram' (I,i,88–9).

Iago's dislike of women in general is apparent from his exchange with Desdemona as they wait on Cyprus for the arrival of Othello's ship. He is witty but cynical: 'you are pictures out a'doors, / Bells in your parlors, wild-cats in your kitchens, / Saints in your injuries, devils being offended, / Players in your huswifery, and huswives in your beds. / . . . You rise to play, and go to bed to work' (II,i,109–12, 115).[105] Even the best woman is good only 'To suckle fools and chronicle small beer' (II,i,160). For Desdemona this opinion represents a 'most lame and impotent conclusion!' (II,i,161); she appeals to gallant Cassio for a rebuttal.

Clearly Iago feels inferior to Cassio, the man who has been promoted over him and who is, in the ensign's own words, 'a proper man, . . . [one] fram'd to make women false' (I,iii,392, 398). Part of the 'daily beauty' in his rival's life (V,i,19) is Cassio's ease and success with women. A ladies' man, the lieutenant finds real the soldier's fantasy. He is 'almost [but not quite] damn'd in a fair wife' (I,i,21) – that is, having all the women he wants without having to marry any of them.

Othello, too, though foreign and older has managed to woo, win, and marry the fair daughter of a Venetian Senator. Iago's taunting of the Moor about Desdemona's supposed infidelity is an expression of his profound inner jealousy. To compensate for his feeling of inferiority, he sets out to destroy the loving relationship. He stabs Othello with obscene daggers: 'Would you . . . / Behold her topp'd?' (III,iii,395–6). He creates an imaginary scene to drive the Moor wild with jealousy: they 'kiss in private', she 'be naked with her friend in bed', he lies 'With her? On her; what you will' (IV,i,2,3,34). Iago's diction is often bawdy, and his figurative language seems obsessively concerned with female and generative references: 'my Muse labors, / And thus she is deliver'd' (II,i,127–8), 'There are many events in the womb of time which will be deliver'd' (I,iii,369–70), and his plan 'is engend'red. Hell and night/Must bring this monstrous birth to the world's light' (I,iii,403–4).

What, then, does all this elaboration of Iago's attitudes toward and relationships with women have to do with Shakespeare's Venetian setting in *Othello*? Along with its other arcane fascinations, Venice in the early seventeenth century, according to J. W. Stoye, was 'home of the . . . homosexual'.[106] Moryson, for one, observed in person the 'fierce affections to forbidden lusts, and to those most which are most forbidden'.[107] Nashe, too, writes of Italian 'Sodomitrie'.[108] Shakespeare's *Richard II* possibly and Marlowe's *Edward II* surely treated the subject of homosexuality on the Renaissance stage. Venice is a suggestive backdrop for presenting a subject that a number of scholars have seen at work in *Othello*.[109]

It would seem that Iago is motivated not only by what he himself recognizes, but also by what he has repressed. He wounds Cassio significantly in a leg (V,i,28); he delights in thinking about 'many worthy and chaste dames . . . [who] (All guiltless) meet reproach' (IV,i,46–7). The imagined dream which Iago recounts to Othello as another 'proof' of Desdemona's infidelity is blatant with overtones of homosexual wish-fulfilment:

> . . . I lay with Cassio lately, . . .
> In sleep I heard him say, "Sweet Desdemona,
> Let us be wary, let us hide our loves";
> And then, sir, would he gripe and wring my hand;
> Cry, "O Sweet creature!" then kiss me hard,
> As if he pluck'd up kisses by the roots
> That grew upon my lips; then laid his leg
> Over my thigh, and sigh'd, and kiss'd, and then
> Cried, "Cursed fate that gave thee to the Moor!"
>
> (III,iii,413–26)

Iago cannot tolerate joyous heterosexual love and seeks to destroy it wherever he can.

If the Venetian background of *Othello* helps to suggest Iago's homosexuality, it also plays some tricks on expectation. As a courtesan, Bianca should be indifferent to her client Cassio, but instead has fallen in love with him. Sophisticated Venetian ladies like Desdemona, by English tradition and reputation, were supposed to be unfaithful to their husbands. Brabantio's parting shot is: 'Look to her, Moor, if thou hast eyes to see;/She has deceiv'd her father, and may thee' (I,iii,292–3). But Desdemona turns out to be a true and loyal wife. Finally, though the Venetian Iago displays intense jealousy and a desire for the harshest revenge, so too does the Moor more sensationally in Shakespeare's play, and this innocent abroad is not even an Italian.

3
The Terra Firma

'Learning teacheth more in one yeare', writes Roger Ascham back from nine days in Venice, 'than experience in twentie: And learning teacheth safelie when experience maketh mo miserable than wise. He hazardeth sore, that waxeth wise by experience'.[1] Here is the impassioned cry of the Protestant moralist warning of the dangers of travel to the new Italy, a land fallen from its former glory: '*Italie* now, is not that *Italie*, that it was wont to be: . . . Vertue once made that contrie Mistres over all the worlde. Vice now maketh that contrie slave to them, that before, were glad to serve it.'[2] Ascham cautions his countrymen about the dangers.

The first and most serious is exposure to the Roman religion. If a young gentleman need visit Italy, Ascham advises, it were best he do so 'under the kepe and garde of him, who, by his wisdome and honestie, by his example and authoritie, may be hable to kepe them safe and sound, in the feare of God, [and] in Christes trewe Religion'.[3] The second danger is related to the first – Italian books. Ascham contends that 'Mo Papistes be made, by your mer[r]y bookes of *Italie*, than by your earnest bookes of *Lovain*.'[4] Though the schoolmaster admits he loves the Italian language better than all others excepting Greek and Latin, he is anxious about the collections of popular and lurid Italian tales to be found everywhere. Indeed, Englishmen need not travel to Italy or know Italian to find and read them; translations are 'sold in every shop in London'.[5] On the other side, Ascham praises Hoby's translation of Castiglione's *Il Cortegiano*, 'which booke, advisedlie read, and diligentlie followed, but one yeare at home in England, would do a yong ientleman more good, I wisse, then three yeares travell abrode spent in *Italie*'.[6]

The final danger of Italy is the temptation to embrace bad customs and habits when there, then bring them home. Ascham cites those young men who now are 'contemners of mariage and readie persuaders of all other to the same'.[7] He describes the devil incarnate, the 'Englishman Italianated':

He, that by living, and traveling in *Italie*, bringeth home into

England out of *Italie*, the Religion, the learning, the policie, the experience, the maners of *Italie*. That is to say, for Religion, Papistrie or worse: for learnyng, lesse commonly than they caried out with them: for pollicie, a factious hart, a discoursing head, a mynde to medle in all mens matters: for experience, plentie of new mischieves never knowne in England before: for maners, varietie of vanities, and chaunge of filthy lyving.[8]

Ascham was not the only one to condemn Italian travel. Towards the end of his life, William Cecil, Lord Burghley (to whom *The Scholemaster* is inscribed), instructed the caretakers of his children not to allow them to 'pass the Alps, for they shall learn nothing there [in Italy] but pride, blasphemy, and atheism'.[9] Bishop Hall, too, warned of the 'proud majesty of pompous ceremonies, wherewith the hearts of children and fools are easily taken'.[10] And there were many others of this persuasion.

But there were also those who argued that travel experience was beneficial. Among them, to be sure, was Fynes Moryson. He writes as if in specific answer to Ascham: 'there can hardly bee found a man so blockish, so idle, or so malicious, as to discourage those that thirst after knowledge from not so doing' by travel.[11] Moryson reasons: 'Surely many fall into vices abroad, but more at home; many returning from forraigne parts, after they have abroad satisfied their disordinate appetites, by giving youth his swinge (as the Proverbe is), doe at home cast off their vices, and returne to the old bounds of shamefastnesse, which at home they never violated; adding to their old vertues the luster of forraigne ornaments.'[12]

Shakespeare is on Moryson's side. Like the journalist, the playwright sees travel as educational. His young protagonists must experience the world 'abroad' to mature. From Lucentio to Ferdinand, they leave their native cities to learn, grow, and wive. Perhaps the single exception is Romeo who, except for a brief sojourn in Mantua, matures exclusively at home. But even Romeo comes back from Mantua significantly changed. Shakespeare's women, too, are often shown in foreign places. Julia and Helena, for example, are also travellers.

The 'mer[r]y bookes of *Italie*' that Ascham warns against are some of the very sources for Shakespeare's Italian plays. Shakespeare, however, far from recommending the extravagant fashions, behaviour, or religion of his Italian materials, reinforces homey English values and morality in his plays. In fact, the object of his satire is usually the faddish veneer of the 'foreign'. From the slang of Parolles to the sword play in *Romeo and Juliet*, the novel is suspect when compared with the traditional. Shakespeare's young gentlemen, like Bertram and Proteus, as if to bear out Moryson, return to the fold better and wiser after their youthful flings. Travel is indeed educational.

Padua was the great Italian Renaissance educational centre. Founded in 1222 by Frederick II, 'the famous University of Padoa', by Shakespeare's time, might only be 'The third for antiquity, but [it was the] cheefe for dignity.'[13] Moryson explains that Venice had subdued the city of Padua in 1405, and subsequently 'did amplify the University with priviledges and many ornaments'.[14] Among student benefits was the waiver of certain taxes: 'My selfe retorning from Padoa towardes England, and having the testimony of the university (vulgarly called Matricola) that I was a Student thereof was thereby freed from many small payments.'[15] And in Padua a student could get away with murder quite literally: 'uppon priviledges of the University . . . murther in schollers is punished only by banishment'.[16]

The University at Padua was especially reputed as a medical school. Among the more notable English physicians who studied there were John Caius (who gave his name to the Cambridge College), doctor to Edward VI, Mary, and Elizabeth, and William Harvey, who first described the circulation of the blood early in the seventeenth century. The famous anatomy theatre, still preserved today, dates from 1594.

But Padua was more than a medical school. At one time or another Dante, Petrarch, and Tasso studied there. Like Shakespeare's Lucentio, the great Galileo left the confining atmosphere of Pisa for Padua; he lectured at the University from 1592 to 1610. Under the protection of the Venetian state, and thus free from the tide of Renaissance Italian religious repression due to papal and clerical influence, the University was an intellectual island in a stormy sea of general intolerance. Because it enjoyed comparative freedom of inquiry, it became an especially appealing place for foreigners – especially ones of the Protestant persuasion. When William Thomas stopped at Padua in about the middle of the sixteenth century, he learned 'the number of scholars was little less than fifteen hundred'.[17] By the beginning of the seventeenth century, this number had swollen to about 6000. Sir Henry Wotton, ambassador at Venice for James I, remarks the English students among them: 'our English swarme at Padua'.[18]

In *The Taming of the Shrew*, Lucentio's picture of the Lombard region of Italy as 'fruitful . . . , / The pleasant garden of great Italy' (I,i,3–4) may owe something to Florio's *Second Frutes*, but in any case it seems the standard description for this part of the country as one can see from Thomas Coryat: 'as Italy is the garden of the World, so is Lombardy the garden of Italy'.[19] As for the city of Padua itself, Coryat is typically lavish with his praise: one would think Padua 'Paradise' if one did not know otherwise, 'For indeed it is as sweetly seated as any place of the whole world is or can be.'[20] The city of Pisa is twice mentioned in *The Taming of the Shrew* as 'renowned for grave citizens' (I,i,10; IV,ii,95). This is typical of the kind of evocative but vague detail that Shakespeare uses in his Italian dramas at the expense of, say, leaning towers.

Though not renowned as a university centre, Verona like Padua had at least some literary reputation for learning among the English. Anthony Munday writes in *Zelauto* (1580) of its *'Accademies . . . woorthily governed, and . . . schollers so effectually instructed.'*[21] 'O, what learning is!' exclaims the Nurse (III,iii,160). But Romeo will have nothing of 'Adversity's sweet milk, philosophy' (III,iii,55) when he is banished from Verona: 'Hang up philosophy! / Unless philosophy can make a Juliet, / Displant a town, reverse a prince's doom, / It helps not, it prevails not' (III,iii,57–60).

Verona's antiquity and connections with ancient Rome comprised its real Renaissance reputation. Arthur Brooke's *Romeus and Juliet*, Shakespeare's source poem, begins with a description of the city:

There is beyonde the Alps, a towne of aunciect fame
Whose bright renoune yet shineth cleare, Verona men it
    name,
Bylt in an happy time, bylt on a fertile soyle,
Maynteined by the heavenly fates, and by the townish toyle.
The fruitfull hilles above, the pleasant vales below,
The silver streame with chanell depe, that through the towne
    doth flow,
The store of springes that serve for use, and eke for ease
And other moe commodities which profite may and please,
Eke many certaine signes of thinges betyde of olde,
To fyll the hungry eyes of those that curiously beholde

Doe make this towne to be preferde above the rest
Of Lumbard townes, or at least compared with the best.[22]

Moryson, with unusual poetic reach, saw Verona as 'built in the forme of a Lute, the necke whereof lies towards the West, on which side the River Athesis . . . doth not only compasse the City, but runs almost through the center of the body of this Lute'.[23] He goes on to describe the 'many ruines of an old Theater' and the 'wall of bricke' encompassing the city.[24] Yet Shakespeare, as he does with his other Italian settings, treats Verona generally, failing to mention its famous amphitheatre ruins, or even its river. Verona is noted passingly as 'old' in *The Taming of the Shrew* (I,ii,49), and in *Romeo and Juliet* its fairness (Pr. 2) and 'ancient citizens' (I,i,92) is remarked; it has 'streets' (III,i,89) and 'walls' (III,iii,17). Obviously this could describe almost any other city, certainly London. The touches in *Romeo and Juliet* that are more precise and specific – references to 'Old Freetown' and Prince Escalus – came to Shakespeare with his sources. Brooke names Capulet's castle as 'Freetown' and Painter's version of the Romeo and Juliet story mentions 'Lord Bartholomew of Escala', 'Signor Escala'.[25]

The city of Mantua, Castiglione's birthplace, is the other setting in *Romeo and Juliet*. Only a single scene is laid here (V,i), the one in which banished Romeo receives the mistaken information that Juliet is dead and so buys poison from an apothecary in order to return home and die by her side. As with his Veronese setting, Shakespeare took Mantua from his Brooke source. The impoverished apothecary is mentioned in the poem, and noted also is 'the cities lawe [that] forbiddeth him to sell' poison (l. 2574). The Nurse recalls gratuitously that when she weaned Juliet her parents were 'at Mantua' (I,iii,28). In *The Taming of the Shrew*, Hortensio becomes the musician Litio 'born in Mantua' (II,i,60), and the Pendant is also 'Of Mantua' (IV,ii,77). *The Two Gentlemen of Verona*, which shares the Brooke source with *Romeo and Juliet*, contains an outlaw banished 'from Mantua' (IV,i,48) for murdering a gentleman; Silvia seeks Valentine at Mantua in the same play. Conveniently located between Verona and Milan, Mantua seems a place to be from or go to, but Shakespeare, as by now we have come to expect, never mentions any of its history or physical characteristics. Coryat describes Mantua as 'one of the auncientest cites of Italy', and is struck by its fortifications and beauty: 'This Citie is marveilous, and walled round about with faire bricke wals, wherein there are eight gates, and is thought to be four miles in compasse: the buildings both publique and private are very sumptous and magnificent: their streets straite and very spacious. Also I saw many stately Pallaces of a goodly height: it is most sweetly seated in respect of the marvailous sweete ayre thereof, the abundance of goodly meadows, pastures, vineyards, orchards, and gardens about it.'[26]

Though they are *'of* Verona', the scene for most of the two gentlemen's action is in or about Milan – beyond, that is, the Venetian *terra firma*. Shakespeare's Milan is pictured a sophisticated place, apt for lessons in courtesy. Milan was, in fact, a city, in the words of E. S. Bates, 'recognised as unsurpassed as a school . . . for the accomplishments that befitted a gentleman'.[27] It was under Spanish domination during Shakespeare's day, but there is little inkling of this fact in the play. Only mention of a *'Don* Alphonso' (I,iii,39) and *'Don* Antonio' (II,iv,54; italics mine) is in any way suggestive.

Thomas thought the Milan area particularly lovely: 'such another piece of ground for beautiful cities and towns, for goodly rivers, fields, and pastures, and for plenty of flesh, fowl, fresh water fish, grain, wine, and fruits is not to be found again in all our familiar regions'.[28] A century later, John Evelyn saw Milan itself 'one of the princliest Cities in *Europe*, it has no suburbs but is circld with a stately Wall for 10 miles, in the Center of a Country that seems to flow with milk & hony: The aire is excellent, the fields fruitfull to admiration . . .'.[29] Evelyn also admired the architecture of the city, but Thomas was generally unimpressed as compared with what he found in Venice, Florence, or Rome. Thomas does, however, acknowledge the Duomo of Milan, 'one of the rarest works of our time'.[30] Shakespeare does not even remark Milan's Cathedral in his plays.

In sum, if the travel writers always seem to describe the general beauty of the regions and cities belonging to the *terra firma*, the playwright is similarly evocative though virtually devoid of the precise geographical detail of the journalists. It is with touches of character, custom, allusion, and contemporary reputation that the playwright offers his version of the cities Venice ruled. Most importantly, Verona and Padua, and Milan beyond the Signory, are schools of learning and experience for Shakespeare's youthful characters.

A THE TAMING OF THE SHREW

Neither George Gascoigne's *Supposes*, a definite source for *The Taming of the Shrew*, nor *The Taming of A Shrew*, a possible source or version of Shakespeare's play, is set in Padua.[31] *Supposes* is located in Ferrara, near Padua and similarly in the Venetian orbit. *A Shrew's* setting is Athens, associated with Aristotle and Plato, and the seat of ancient learning. With Padua, it is as if Shakespeare combined the suggestions of the two plays' settings, one Italian and the other identified with education, to derive his own locale for *The Taming of the Shrew*.

Litio and Petruchio are servant characters in *Supposes*. The name Petruchio also may have been reinforced as a good Italian name for Shakespeare's character by a person at court, Petruccio Ubaldini. This soldier came to England during the reign of Henry VIII, married an Englishwoman and possibly served Queen Elizabeth as a diplomat. During a long life, he was a visible Italian moving in important English circles.[32] Moryson describes another Petruccio, this one in 'the most Factious Citty of Pistoia', whose story involves a Bianca:

> the sonne of the Chancelor and the sonne of Signor Petruccio, . . . when contending together the sonne of the Chancelor gave a blow on the eare to the other, the Chancelor sent his sonne to Petruccio to crave pardon on his knees, who crueely cutt of his right hand, wher-uppon all the Citty was divided into a long lasting faction, and because the Chancelors wife was named Bianca that faction took the name Bianchi that is the white, and the other took the name of Neri that is the Black.[33]

Besides the coincidence of names with *The Taming of the Shrew*, what is interesting is the hand-severing detail reminiscent of *Titus Andronicus*, the family feud which recalls *Romeo and Juliet*, and the symbolic colours of the factions, like the red and white roses in the Henry VI plays. All of these works by Shakespeare were written, of course, within five or six years of one another.

Venice and not Padua was the economic centre of the Signory (as portrayed, for example, in *The Merchant of Venice* and *Volpone*), so it is perhaps surprising at first to find that Petruchio comes to 'wive it wealthily in Padua' (I,ii,75). However, with this Paduan setting Shakespeare directs his audience to the important central theme of

The Taming of the Shrew – education, the social lessons taught and learned in a purposefully selected university city. Ironically, as Brian Morris observes, 'The play makes clear that the true paths to learning are not those of the school or university. Formal education is contrasted to its detriment against the practical academy of experience.'[34]

There are a number of supposed and real teachers in the play. Lucentio and Hortensio are engaged to be 'schoolmasters' for the two sisters. Disguised as Cambio, Lucentio is presented as a 'young scholar, that hath been long studying at Rheims, [who is] . . . cunning in Greek, Latin, and other languages' (II,i,79–81). As a strategy to woo Bianca, he 'teaches' her 'the Art to Love' (IV,ii,8). Disguised as Litio, Hortensio is supposedly a teacher 'Cunning in music and the mathematics' (II,i,56). He has a terrible time with Kate as a pupil, and enters at one point 'with his head broke' by a lute.

Petruchio 'will be master of what is mine own' (III,ii,229), and in conventional Renaissance fashion views Kate as 'my goods, my chattels', beneath him in the order of things, and thus subservient. Indeed, it is his *responsibility* to tame her. Petruchio's pedagogy has nothing in common with Roger Ascham's spare the rod method as articulated in *The Scholemaster*. Petruchio handles even his own servants roughly (IV,i,148 S.D.), and Grumio's comic instructions to Curtis and the others at the country house (IV,i) are a parody of the master's methods. Petruchio modifies Kate's behaviour by brainwashing.[35] His educational theory is applicable to all underlings, servants, falcons, his wife:

> She [will] eat no meat to-day, nor none shall eat;
> Last night she slept not, nor to-night she shall not;
> As with the meat, some undeserved fault
> I'll find about the making of the bed,
> And here I'll fling the pillow, there the bolster,
> This way the coverlet, another way the sheets.
> Ay, and amid this hurly I intend
> That all is done in reverend care of her,
> And in conclusion, she shall watch all night,
> And if she chance to nod I'll rail and brawl,
> And with the clamor keep her still awake.
> This is a way to kill a wife with kindness,
> And thus I'll curb her mad and headstrong humor.
>
> (IV,i,197–209)

Petruchio also teaches Kate by example – if she will be perverse, he will be more so to demonstrate how miserable perversity is. When Kate strikes Petruchio, he tells her he will 'cuff' her back if she strikes him again (II,i,220). He comes late to their wedding and in bizarre apparel, forces his bride to depart with him before the wedding supper, insures her awful trip to his country house and, when there, will not let her have her way in anything. Even reverence for religion falls before Petruchio's taming plan: at the wedding Petruchio is quoted as swearing loudly, 'Ay, by gogswouns, . . . / That all amaz'd the priest let fall the book, / And as he stoop'd again to take it up, / This mad-brain'd bridegroom took him such a cuff / That down fell priest and book, and book and priest' (III,ii,160–4).

Petruchio similarly does not honour conventional social decorum when it serves to make a point with his wife: Kate must kiss him in public on the street (V,i,143–50). By the end, however, Petruchio's thorough 'taming-school' (IV,ii,54) has taught Kate how to entreat (IV,iii,7), and that one is responsible for one's own moods and actions (IV,i,174).

According to Steeven Guazzo's *Civile Conversation*, a popular courtesy book (translated in 1581 and 1586), 'it is a monstrous and naughtye thing, to see a Gyrle use suche libertye and boldenesse in her Gesture, lookes, and talke, as is proper to men: therefore lette maydes learne in all their behavioure to express that modesty, which is so seemely for their estate'.[36] Because Kate learns her lesson well, she can become the teacher for her sister Bianca and the 'wealthy widow' near the end of the play. Kate's graceful lecture on wifely duty forwards the traditional notion that women are subservient to men in God's perfect scheme of things. The disobedience to their husbands displayed by Bianca and the widow shows that they need the reformed Kate's instruction.

Besides Kate, there are a number of other learners in *The Taming of the Shrew*. Observing Cambio's success with Bianca, Hortensio determines that 'Kindness in women, not their beauteous looks, / Shall win my love' (IV,ii,41–2). He will marry the 'wealthy widow', and enroll in Petruchio's 'taming-school' (IV,ii,50–4) in order to learn how 'To tame a shrew and charm her chattering tongue' (IV,ii,58). Hortensio's encounter with the reformed Kate causes him to exclaim that if his widow 'be froward, / Then [Petruchio] hast . . . taught Hortensio to be untoward' (IV,v,78–9). The cure for lovesickness in *Euphues* is the pursuit of learning ('Love gives place to labour, labour and thou shalt never love'), but Lucentio turns things around. He has come to Padua to study 'Virtue' and 'happiness', 'To suck the sweets of sweet philosophy' (I,i,18, 19, 28); however, he has fallen in love and is diverted. His more formal education is abandoned. Yet father Vincentio, after fearing (like most fathers) his son and servant 'spend all at the university' (V,i,69–70), learns that Lucentio's informal education has been practical and successful. He approves of his son's wife. Baptista Minola, too, has been duped by his child Bianca but with happy results. The Pedant is a literal student in Padua, and is also duped.

Petruchio's learning experience is the most subtle in the play. Traditionally wealth as well as birth were important for social place, and Petruchio comes abroad wishing to add to the riches left him by his dead father. Shakespeare is correct in assuming that in Italy a large dowry might be the reward for marrying a less desirable woman. Moryson writes that 'in the Provinces of the State of Venice [which would include Padua], . . . they were wont to marry their virgins . . . to him that would give most for them, and by the money given for the fayrest, raysed dowrys for them that were ill favored'.[37] Thus Petruchio is concerned at first with the shrew's dowry not her person. He has 'thrust' himself 'into this maze, / Happily to wive and thrive' (I,ii,55–6), and he wants 'One rich enough to be Petruchio's wife / (As wealth is burthen of my wooing dance)' (I,ii,67–8). He is in a hurry too: 'my business asketh haste, / And every day I cannot come to woo' (II,i,114–15). But this bluster from Petruchio can easily obscure another explicit reason why he has set out from Verona: 'home [is] / Where small experience grows' (I,ii,58); he has, therefore, 'come abroad to see the world' (I,ii,58). Beyond his posturing for Kate, Petruchio has noticeable rough edges to his character which ask refinement. He is overly proud. To Gremio he brags:

> Have I not in my time heard lions roar?
> Have I not heard the sea, puff'd up with winds,
> Rage like an angry boar chafed with sweat?
> Have I not heard great ordnance in the field,
> And heaven's artillery thunder in the skies?
> Have I not in a pitched battle heard
> Loud 'larums, neighing steeds, and trumpets' clang?
> And do you tell me of a woman's tongue, . . .
> Tush, tush, fear boys with bugs.
> (I,ii,200–10)

He is so quarrelsome with his servant Grumio that his friend Hortensio must ask 'patience' of him (I,ii,45). He seems overly self-confident, as when Baptista Minola asks how his wooing is progressing and he responds: 'It were impossible I should speed amiss' (II,i,283). Clearly much of Petruchio's character in relation to Kate is only an act to change her behaviour. Yet his statement toward the end of the play, '"tis the mind that makes the body rich' (IV,iii,172), suggests some self-realization on Petruchio's part as well as a lesson for Kate. Petruchio has come to Padua 'to wive it wealthily' (I,ii,75), but has learned that 'wealthily' means more than material riches. Petruchio has found real love and a perfect wife in the reformed Kate. The irony is that he receives more than a usual dowry for his efforts. He gets extra money from Gremio and Hortensio for wooing Kate in the first place, receives a supplemental dowry from Baptista Minola for Kate's 'new' and changed self, and still more payoff after winning the wager at the end of the play.

The Taming of the Shrew contains many words and phrases associated with pedagogy. There are schoolmasters and tutors and pedants who instruct, teach, give lessons to studious pupils or scholars from books or not. 'O this learning, what a thing it is!' (I,ii,159), exclaims Gremio (gulled by Lucentio's schoolmaster disguise). Lessons are often delivered to characters and audience in proverbial phrases: 'No profit grows where is no pleasure ta'en' (I,i,39); 'nothing comes amiss, so money comes withal' (I,ii,81–2); 'where two raging fires meet together, / They do consume the thing that feeds their fury' (II,i,132–3); 'To me she's married, not unto my clothes' (III,ii,117); 'Better once than never, for never too late' (V,i,150); '"Tis a good hearing when children are toward, / But a harsh hearing when women are froward' (V,ii,182–3). John Florio's well-known contemporary manuals for learning the Italian language (*First Fruites* and *Second Frutes*, 1578, 1591) abound with proverbs; indeed, they are one of the dominant features of Florio's writing style. John Eliot's satiric *Orthoepia Gallica* (1593) mocks Florio specifically in this area.[38] Perhaps, therefore, Shakespeare connected Italian pedagogy with proverbial lessons.

Travel is educational, and, since Shakespeare's play is centrally about learning, we might expect to find a number of travellers in it. As noted earlier, 'home' is limiting; it is the place, in Petruchio's words, 'Where small experience grows'. In the Induction, the Lord hears trumpets at his house and speculates that the sound signals the party of 'some noble gentleman . . . / (Travelling some journey)'

(Ind. i,75–6). In the play proper, Lucentio, born in Pisa and brought up in Florence, now journeys to Padua. His father Vincentio travels from Pisa to Padua to seek him out. Most travelled of all though, significantly, is the Pedant. Originally from Mantua, his destinations include Rome and Tripoli (IV,ii,75–6); he has 'bills for money by exchange/From Florence' (IV,ii,89–90). (Shakespeare writes knowingly here of Florence's reputation as a banking centre.[39]) There are also other realistic touches relating to travel in the play. Renaissance tourists were always fearful of breaking some unknown law (see V,i,81–2) and abuse of foreigners by natives was common (see V,i,108). Of course, travellers were likely butts for jokes as well (see IV,v,71–3).

There are a number of accurate items of Italian local colour to be found in the play. Right at the start, Lucentio describes Padua as 'nursery of arts' (I,i,2). Moryson writes that the University is, for instance, 'an excellent place to learne and practise the Art of Musicke'.[40] Hortensio is thus credible as a music teacher in Padua. Venice is correctly identified as the place for fashion. Petruchio 'will unto Venice/To buy apparel 'gainst . . . [his] wedding-day' (II,i,314–15). Obviously there is broad satire intended by Shakespeare when Petruchio shows up for the wedding 'in a new hat and an old jerkin; a pair of old breeches thriced turn'd; a pair of boots that have been candle-cases, one buckled, another lac'd' (III,ii,43–6). We recall that Jaques in *As You Like It*, who has also been in Venice, wears 'strange suits' (IV,i,34). Among much else Gremio promises for Bianca's hand is a 'Valens of Venice gold' (II,i,354).

According to Petruchio, Kate's initial cursedness is merely 'for policy' (II,i,292); after the marriage the new husband begins his so-called reign 'politicly' (IV,i,188). This diction has Italian connotations, as craftiness was considered to be typical of the Italian character steeped in government. Bits and snatches of the Italian language, too, are attempts to authenticate and enrich the Italian flavour of the play (see I,i,25,198; I,ii,24–6,278,280;IV,ii,63). These words and phrases are sometimes imprecisely rendered versions of familiar and copybook Italian; hence, Shakespeare betrays no real knowledge of the Italian language. Gremio is twice referred to as a 'pantaloon' (I,i,47 S.D.; III,i,37), suggesting the origin of his character type in the *Commedia dell'arte*.

Shakespeare has been accused of getting wrong a number of his facts about Italy in *The Taming of the Shrew*. First and foremost, Padua is not a city in the Lombard region as it is usually defined. Neither is it a seaport, as many have pointed out. Lucentio's 'come ashore' (I,i,42), or Hortensio's question to Petruchio: 'what happy gale / Blows you to Padua here from old Verona?' (I,ii,48–9) might suggest that Shakespeare thought it was. But the friends may be using figurative not literal language, and one need not read the exchange as necessarily referring to a boat trip on water. Petruchio employs another nautical metaphor when speaking of the Kate he has yet to meet: 'I will board her though she chide as loud / As thunder when the clouds in autumn crack' (I,ii,95–6). And he reports that he has 'heard the sea puff'd up with winds' (I,ii,201). Though from inland Verona, clearly Petruchio has had some seafaring experience, perhaps as a soldier (see I,ii,203–6). Another supposed error by Shakespeare is the identification of Tranio's father as 'a sailmaker in Bergamo' (V,i,77–8). A landlocked city, Bergamo, it is argued, would not have sailmakers. On the other hand, J. W. Draper speculates that 'perhaps its present fame for the manufacture of textiles goes back to the sixteenth century, and may explain Shakespeare's reference'.[41] The family 'Bentivolii' (I,i,13) was actually Bolognese not Pisan as in the play.

The playwright may be describing *ossa bucco* when Grumio refers to a 'neat's foot' meal for Kate, and 'fat tripe finely broiled' also sounds like an Italian dish (IV,iii,17,20). However, 'a piece of beef and mustard' (IV,iii,23) is surely English. Petruchio's 'country house', so called by Pope and later editors, is decidedly rustic English in character. The servants are named Curtis, Joseph, Philip, Adam, Rafe, and so on. 'Long-lane' (IV,iii,185) is an English street designation, the 'Pegasus' an English not Genoese-sounding Inn (IV,iv,5). The sleeve of Kate's would-be dress is 'carv'd like an apple-tart' (IV,iii,89), an English sweet. And snatches of various English ballads are sung in the play.

In *The Taming of the Shrew*, Petruchio is at first a kind of special knight come to free the beautiful princess Bianca from the shrewish witch Kate who is keeping the younger sister from her destiny. But unlike the traditional prince in the story, Petruchio gets the witch and not the princess as his reward – he 'Achieve[s] the elder, set[s] the younger free' (I,ii,266). Kate, though, is of course more a sleeping beauty than a witch. Enchanted by her own shrewish posturing, she must kiss Petruchio – 'Kiss me Kate' – and awaken to her 'true self', an obedient and gentle one.

Kate's awakening in the play proper is played against Christopher

Sly's drunken slumbering in the Induction in order to make a point about the nature of dramatic illusion as well as the obvious one about wifely duty. Christopher Sly believes he is a lord because what he takes to be the reality around him supports this notion. An audience believes in the 'truth' of plays like *The Taming of the Shrew*, 'a kind of history' (Ind. ii,141), because it willingly suspends its disbelief and so becomes involved in the presented fiction. Even the Italy seems real. Shakespeare's play is replete with disguises, dupings, poses, etc., and such 'drama' inevitably raises reflexive questions in the thoughtful spectator. The Induction serves as a variation of the familiar Renaissance English play prologue which characteristically asks an audience's indulgence and imagination. Instead of the usual chorus, however, directing an audience to, say, 'the vasty fields of France', Shakespeare comically dramatizes an audience imagining by way of Christopher Sly. The seduction of Sly by the 'real' Lord parallels the audience's seduction by the dramatist (also, possibly, the seduction of the English by Italy). The change in setting from the Induction (Stratford and Burton Heath) to the play proper (Padua and Verona) is very deliberate. The movement is from the familiar to the remote, the commonplace to the foreign, the real to the fictional.

Both audience and Christopher Sly are presented with a play. It is a grand joke that this play about wifely duty is designed to prevent Sly from intimacy with his supposed 'wife', and the audience is also kept from whatever 'home duty' by watching the play. The setting is Italy – that upside-down world to Shakespeare's English. If Kate comes to 'believe' the moon is the sun because Petruchio tells her so, Shakespeare's audience as well comes to believe in the fiction of the play as it gives itself up to the 'counterfeit supposes' (V,i,117) of the playwright and the actors. The audience knows that what is seen is not 'real' but, like Christopher Sly at the beginning, it allows itself to be duped by surroundings, settings, costumes – it is drawn into the fiction. More alert than Sly if we stay awake for the entire play, we are nonetheless like him as audience. The story may be that Italy is attractive, believable, real for the moment. But Italy's appeal also may be illusion. Thus, the biggest lesson in *The Taming of the Shrew* turns out to be for Shakespeare's audience.

B ROMEO AND JULIET

Notwithstanding Shakespeare's fogginess about both Mantua and Verona in *Romeo and Juliet*, a number of commentators have felt an authentic Italian ambience in the play. Lucy Simpson claims that 'no play more strikingly illustrated Italian life and influence'.[42] Mario Praz, too, felt it 'much stronger in local color than [for example] *The Two Gentlemen of Verona*'.[43] Praz also observes that the poetry in *Romeo and Juliet* harkens back to characteristically Italian forms and techniques: 'Romeo's love expresses itself in the metaphors of the school of Serafino Aquilano.'[44] More obviously, complete sonnets as well as sonnet parts are embedded in the play. Finally, A. C. Partridge believes, 'the theme of Shakespeare's *Romeo and Juliet* is the nearest in conception to the art of the Italian Renaissance'.[45]

Some of Shakespeare's details are authentic. Moryson reports the masque parties at 'Carnival Time': 'Yea the very houses of noblemen and gentlemen, upon occasions of meetings to danse with wemen and virgins of honour, are open for any masked persons to enter and behold them.'[46] This describes accurately the Capulet party found in *Romeo and Juliet*. And, though detention after exposure to contagious illness was a common practice throughout Europe, Friar John's quarantine corresponds with Moryson's details about Italian regulations: 'They are carefull to avoyde infection of the plague, and to that purpose in every City have magistrates for health. So as in tymes of danger when any Citty in or neare Italy is infected, travelers cannot passe by land except they bring a bolletino or certificate of their health from the place whence they come, and otherwise must make la quarantina or tryall of forty days for their health in a lazaretto or hospitall for that purpose.'[47] Coryat found Italian burial customs 'strange'.[48] Unlike the English, aristocratic Italians were often buried in family tombs. Friar Lawrence tells Juliet 'the manner of our country': 'Thou shalt be borne to that same ancient vault / Where all the kindred of the Capulets lie' (IV,i,111–12). Moryson observes that 'through all Italy, they are not buryed in severall graves digged of purpose, as commonly with us, but in Caves or vaults, either private to their Familyes, or common to the people. And they are buried in their apparrell, and have their faces covered with linnen, and the bodyes are cast into the Cave, which is presently made up very close, because as some of the dead bodyes are consumed, so others are more or less rotten as they have been longer or latter buryed, from the stincke whereon they feare

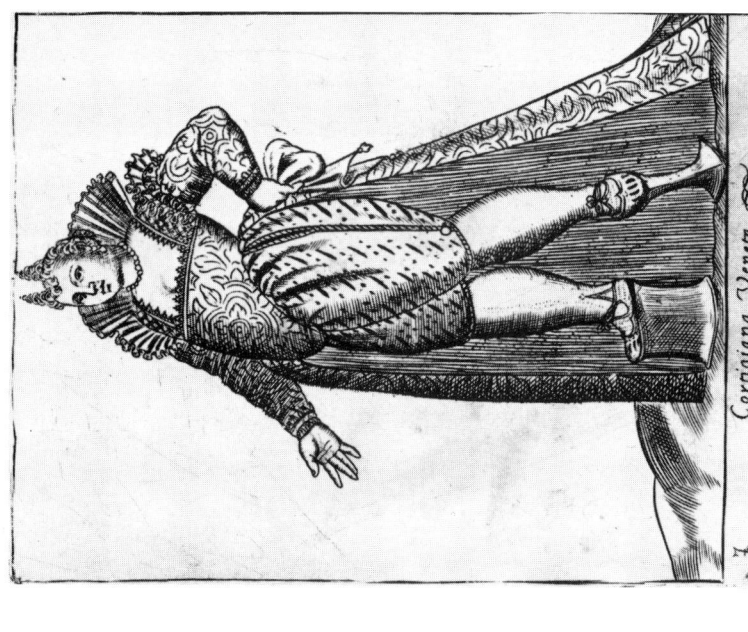

1b Venetian courtesan wearing chapineys. From Pietro Bertelli, *Diversarum nationum habitus*, vol. 1, 1594.

1a Coryat and courtesan. From Thomas Coryat. *Coryat's Crudities*, 1611.

2 'The Description of Venice'. From Fynes Moryson, *An Itinerary*, 1617. Important places are indicated by letters on the map. For example, A. 'The great channell', B. 'The market place of Saint Marke . . .', C. 'The Cathedrall Church of Saint Peter . . .', etc.

3 Rialto bridge. From Pietro Bertelli, *Diversarum nationum habitus*, vol. 3, 1596.

4a Venetian merchant.

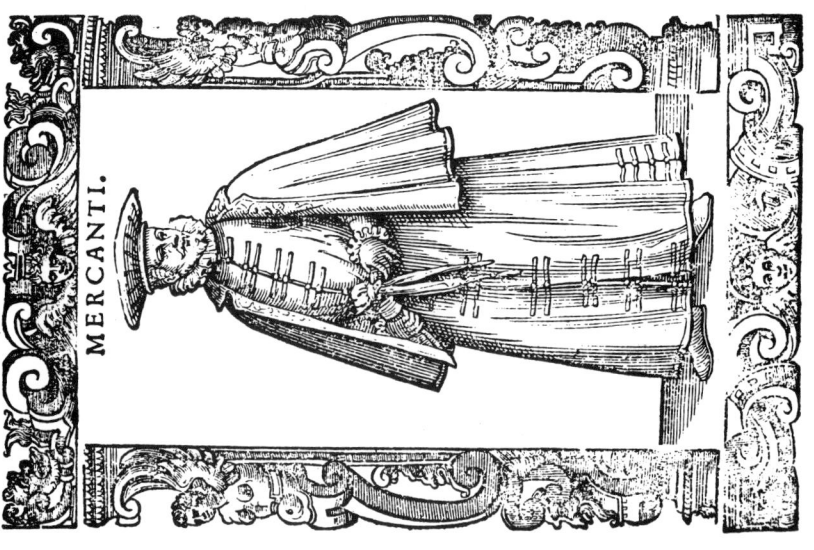

4b Noble moor.

From Cesare Vecellio, *Degli habiti antichi et moderni*, 1590.

George Silver his

TO know the perfect length of your Sword, you shall stand with your sword and dagger drawn, as you see this picture, keeping out straight your dagger arme, drawing backe your sword as far as conueniently you can, not opening the elbow ioynt of your sword arme: and looke what you can draw within your dagger, that is the iust length of your sword, to be made according to your owne stature.

If the sword be longer, you can hardly vncrosse backe with your feet. If shorter, then you can hardly make a true crosse without putting in of your feet, the which times are too long to answer the time of the hand.

The like reasons for the short staffe, half Pike, Forrest bill, Partisan, or Gleue, or such like weapons of perfect length.

5 Sword and dagger. From George Silver, *Paradoxes of Defence*, 1599.

6 Milan. From Georg Braun, *Civitates orbis terrarum*, 1572. Note St. Gregory's Well, the square structure on the right of the map beyond the city walls.

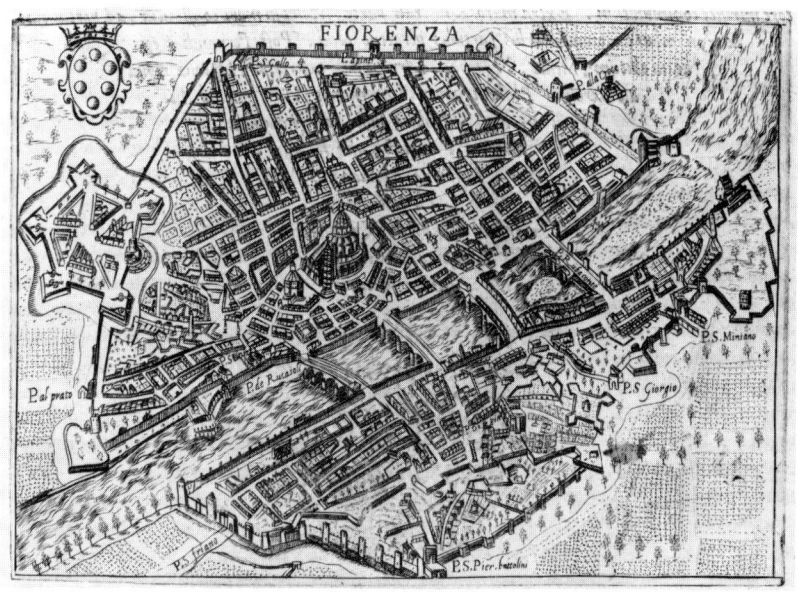

7a (above) Florence. From Pietro Bertelli, *Theatrum urbium Italicarum*, 1599.
7b (below) Siena. From Georg Braun, *Civitates orbis terrarum*, 1572.

8 'The Battle of Lepanto'. Anonymous artist.

infection'.[49] Other Italian details in *Romeo and Juliet* include references to Petrarch and Laura (II,iv,39), and the Castiglionean advice to Romeo to compare his love Rosaline with other beauties as a way of assuaging his desire for her.

Then there are the details of supposed Italian temperament. Tybalt's irrational rage at his inherited enemy is an example. Another is Romeo's excessive passion for Rosaline at the beginning of the play. His later hyperbolic reaction to his banishment from Juliet would be yet a third. In this latter instance, he appeals to the Friar: 'Hadst thou no poison mix'd, no sharp-ground knife, / No sudden mean of death' (III,iii,44–5)? To be sure, revenge is associated with an Italian setting. As are feuds among families.

Ascham's general condemnation of Italy includes the 'private contention in many families, [and] open factions in every Citie'.[50] Feuding Italian families hired retainers (so-called 'bravoes', 'braves', or 'bravi') to fight their battles, and the law often winked at questions of legality concerning family honour. Coryat describes 'certaine desperate and resolute villaines' in Venice: 'They wander abroad very late in the night to and fro for their prey, like hungry Lyons, being armed with a privy coat of maile, a gauntlet upon their right hand, and a little sharp dagger called a stiletto.'[51] Much as with modern inner-city 'gangs', sections of a city 'belonged' to one group or another; these areas would be fought over periodically. Assassination in the best manner of contemporary gang-land slaying was thought of then as now as typically 'Italian'. Moryson reports almost conventionality obtaining with the personal feud, a tradition so much an accepted part of the culture:

> My selfe at Syenna sawe two gentlemen fall at defiance in the streete, who having each his sworde and Gauntlett, yet agreed to goe home and take more Complete Armes, and then to retourne to fight, not in the fielde, but (forsooth) in the markett place . . . : sargants (whom they could not but expect) came to parte the fray, and Carry them to the governour. Then for many dayes, till the governours could take up the quarrell, these gentlemen with some hundreths of Armed followers . . . walked the streets.[52]

Moryson also gives accounts of various factious families, some siding with Emperor or Pope, Spain or France, etc. He notes the Guelphs and Gibellines, Adorni and Fregosi, Neri and Bianchi, and Cancellieri and Panzodici. 'In generall these names of factions have beene extinguished in processe of tyme, but to this day the Familyes under other names retayne the old hatred, and are very suspitious one of the other, and ready to offer mutuall injuryes.'[53]

The Montague and Capulet feud depicted in *Romeo and Juliet* may or may not be historically true. It is thought by some to date from thirteenth-century political events in Verona during the rule of Bartolommeo della Scala (d. 1304). Luigi da Porto wrote a version of the Romeo and Juliet story in 1530, suggesting that the events took place in 1302; Corte's 1594 history of Verona follows da Porto.[54] Dante mentions the Montecchi and Capelletti dissension as an example of civil disorder in *Purgatorio* (l. 107). What is interesting in the light of today's tourist industry in Verona centred upon Juliet (her tomb, house, and balcony) but not Romeo is the fact that only the historical family Montecchi lived in Verona; the Capelletti were originally a Cremonese family.

There is also an item of English historical interest. Shakespeare's patron Southampton traced his 'ancient blood' back to the Italian Montagues on his mother's side. In a masque written by George Gascoigne for a double wedding in the Dowager Countess' family, a Montague boy-character explains an emblem worn in his cap:

This [is a] token which the Mountacutes dyd beare alwaies,
    for that
They covet to be knowne from Capels where they passe,
From aunclent grutch which lōg ago, 'twene these two
    houses was.[55]

In 1594, around the time of the composition of *Romeo and Juliet*, Southampton concealed in and about his house (Titchfield) two fugitive friends, Charles and Henry Danvers, helping them escape subsequently from England.[56] Henry was wanted in connection with the killing of Henry Long. The Danvers had been feuding with the family of Sir Walter Long, and, in response to the wounding of Charles Danvers, Henry Long was shot dead. A sheriff carrying a warrant for the Danvers was threatened by John Florio of the Southampton household. The Southampton–Montague connection and the episode of the antagonistic families seem to some, including M. C. Bradbrook and New Arden editor Brian Gibbons, more than coincidence. Bradbrook, for example, wonders whether Shakespeare was in attendance at Southampton's coming-of-age party on 6 October 1594, when the Danvers were hiding in his house or close by. Thus, as is usual, a scratch on Shakespeare's Italian surface reveals things English beneath. The thumb-biting among the servants at the beginning of *Romeo and Juliet* (I,i,42–51) may be an Italian gesture, but the characters' subsequent behaviour is that of London apprentices. The street scuffle smacks of a tradesmen battle. The 'Citizens' call to arms is English: 'Clubs, bills, and partisans!' (I,i,73). Though Anthony may be an appropriate Italian servant's name, Potpan, Susan Grindstone, James Soundpost, Simon Catling, and Hugh Rebeck are decidedly English, as are 'join-stools', trenchers, and a 'court-cupboard' (I,v,2,6–7). Snatches of English songs are sung a number of times (II,iv,134–9,144; IV,v,102–7), and some lines of an English poem, 'In Commendation of Musick' by Richard Edwardes (1523–66), are recited (IV,v,126–30). Mercutio's famous Queen Mab speech has roots in English not Italian lore.

From about 1590 onwards, with the arrival of fencing masters from the continent, there was intense English interest in the latest equipment and techniques of swordplay. Italy was again the trendsetter in these matters (though Moryson reports that most Italian cities formally forbade duelling).[57] The fashion was for newer weapons, fancy footwork, and disciplined precision, as against the older and cruder English traditions. In *Paradoxes of Defence* (1599), the Englishman George Silver defends the old ways against the newer methods spelled out in Vincentio Saviolo's *Practice* (1595).[58] 'Fencing . . . in this new fangled age', writes Silver, 'is like our fashions, every daye a change.'[59] Rival Saviolo was a colourful figure in the England of the time, an ambidextrous Paduan who taught dancing as well as duelling, and numbered the Earl of Essex among his many students (both Saviolo's and Silver's books are dedicated to Essex). In a duel, the cumbersome English sword and buckler was no match for the lighter, longer, and more versatile rapier with dagger. A dialogue in John Florio's *First Fruites* derides the buckler as particularly crude: 'What weapon is that buckler?' asks one speaker, to whom the other replies that it is 'A clownish dastardly weapon, and not for a Gentleman.'[60]

In *Romeo and Juliet*, Shakespeare defends the English tradition by way of his sympathetic Italian characters. Benvolio ridicules the *au courant* swordsmanship of Tybalt (I,i,111–12), and Mercutio is even more biting in his contempt: 'He fights as you sing prick-song, keeps time, distance, and proportion; he rests his minim rests, one, two, and the third in your bosom: the very butcher of a silk button, a duellist, a duellist; a gentleman of the very first house, of the first and second cause. Ah, the immortal *passado*, the *punto reverso*, the *hay!'* (II,iv,20–6). Signior Rocco, another of the fencing masters attacked by Silver, was fond of boasting that he could hit an Englishman on any button in a duel. When Mercutio is fatally wounded, he cries out in frustrated anguish: 'a braggart, a rogue, a villain that fights by the book of arithmetic!' (III,i,101–2). Silver contends that luck, not skill or strength, is the main factor in winning with the Italian weapons and discipline.

Like *Othello*, Shakespeare's other Italian tragedy, *Romeo and Juliet* is about an unusual marriage and its consequences. In *Othello*, the marriage between the older black and foreign general and younger white Venetian lady has already taken place before the action begins, but the first act of the play nonetheless has a traditional comic ending: the marriage is affirmed, the father defeated, the daughter successful according to her will. From Act II onward, the focus in the play is on the development of the tragic catastrophe – Iago's duping of Othello and Desdemona's murder and its fallout. Though a clown appears briefly, there is virtually no comedy in *Othello*. *Romeo and Juliet*, on the other hand, is full of comedy. Almost the entire first half of the play is concerned with Romeo's discovery of and marriage to Juliet against all odds. Accompanying this traditionally comic sweep is a range of comic detail. The servants' fight toward the start of the play is the low comedy of physical action, Mercutio's fertile imagination yields witty high comedy, and the soft humour of the friar–gardener's bumbling lies somewhere in between. There are also the scenes with the Nurse and her man Peter, and the servant with the guest list he cannot read. The young gentlemen of the play love bawdy and double entendre. When Juliet wishes 'Three words' (II,ii,142) more of farewell with Romeo during the balcony scene, she talks on for some thirty-four lines!

Like *The Taming of the Shrew*, *Romeo and Juliet* is centrally a learning story. The considered 'philosophy' of the Friar or the common sense lessons of the Nurse, however, are presented as secondary to inner character maturation much greater than any to be found in *The Taming of the Shrew*. Juliet moves from a totally obedient daughter to a woman alone. When the subject of marriage with Paris is broached early in the play, she responds to her mother as an obedient daughter should: 'I'll look to like, if looking liking move;/But no more deep will I endart mine eye / Than your consent gives strength to make it fly' (I,iii,97–9). Later, however, when bigamous marriage with Paris seems imminent and Juliet balks, her father finds her a 'disobedient wretch!' (III,v,160). Eventually she must act out a terrifying drama by herself. The Friar asks if she 'hast the strength of will to slay' herself and 'undertake/A thing like death' (IV,i,72–4). She responds that she can go so far as to

> . . . hide me nightly in a charnel-house,
> O'ercover'd quite with dead men's rattling bones,
> With reeky shanks and yellow chapless skulls;
> Or bid me go into a new-made grave,
> And hide me with a dead man in his shroud –
> Things that, to hear them told, have made me tremble –
> And I will do it without fear or doubt,
> To live an unstain'd wife to my sweet love.
>
> (IV,i,81–8)

Of course, these things are exactly what she must do. Without the guidance of anyone (the Nurse's practical counsel has been rejected), and not really knowing the Friar's motives (perhaps selfish), Juliet agrees to the desperate plan. She is not a capricious young thing anymore; she is now recognized as a mature woman with the courage to act in terms of her love.

Romeo matures too. He moves from his infatuation with and lustful passion for Rosaline early in the play, accompanied by fashionable poses, language, and emotions, to real love and honourable marriage. Despite his spiritual language with Juliet at first meeting, during the balcony scene he complains: 'O, wilt thou leave me so unsatisfied?' (II,ii,125) (to which Juliet responds with surprise: 'What satisfaction canst thou have tonight?' [II,ii,126]). His marriage, duel with Tybalt, and banishment force his coming of age; he must 'be a man' (III,iii,88). When, burdened by catastrophe, he threatens to kill himself, the Friar exclaims, 'Art thou a man? Thy form cries out thou art;/Thy tears are womanish, thy wild acts denote/The unreasonable fury of a beast' (III,iii,109–11). Early in the play Romeo is forever 'lost', and everyone it seems is asking 'Where is Romeo?' But when Romeo returns from Mantua to Verona and the Capulet tomb, alone now and without his friends Mercutio and Benvolio, he is recognizably a 'man'. There has been maturation in Mantua. Paris interrupts while he is opening the tomb, and Romeo's speech is restrained and measured: 'Good gentle *youth*, tempt not a desp'rate *man*' (V,iii,59; italics mine). Before fighting with Paris, he again calls him 'youth' (l. 61) and 'boy' (l. 70). Romeo's 'lightning before death' (V,iii,90) is akin to Hamlet's 'readiness is all' or Edgar's 'ripeness is all' lesson. Romeo has come a long way in a short space, has grown up – just as has Juliet.

The Italian element in *Romeo and Juliet* is rooted in details of contemporary history and custom, and the shared theme of learning and experience common in most of Shakespeare's Italian plays. 'O, what learning is!' exclaims Juliet's nurse, echoing Gremio's earlier cry in *The Taming of the Shrew*, 'O this learning, what a thing it is!'

C THE TWO GENTLEMEN OF VERONA

The Two Gentlemen of Verona shares with *Romeo and Juliet* the Arthur Brooke source, and the Verona and Mantua settings are suggested by the poem. There are also a number of other connections between the tragedy and the comedy resulting from a common source.[61] Both Romeo and Valentine are banished, react to their banishments, and are given advice; there is an impossible rival forwarded by the mistress's father in each play; a rope ladder figures in the two plots; the Third Outlaw's situation in *The Two Gentlemen of Verona* ('Myself was from Verona banished / For practicing to steal away a lady, / An heir, and near allied unto the Duke' [IV,i,45–7]) is similar to Romeo's. 'Julia', a name to be found in the comedy, is close to 'Juliet', from the tragedy, as is 'Mercatio' close to 'Mercutio'. 'Friar Laurence' is mistakenly substituted for 'Friar Patrick' (V,ii,37) in *The Two Gentlemen of Verona*. In *Romeo and Juliet* Shakespeare quotes some lines from a poem by Richard Edwardes, and another source for *The Two Gentlemen of Verona* is thought to be Edwardes' *The Excellent Comedy of Two Most Faithful Friends, Damon and Pithias* (1565). These friends are described as 'two gentlemen of Greece'.[62]

Unlike *Romeo and Juliet*, however, in which Verona is the important central setting, Verona in *The Two Gentlemen* is peripheral; it is portrayed as provincial, a place to get away from. At the beginning of the play, Valentine leaves the city, 'To see the wonders of the world abroad' (I,i,6). Apparently a Veronese citizen, Proteus' uncle contends that 'no travel in . . . youth [is a] great impeachment to . . . age' (I,iii,15–16); fellow native Antonio agrees: one 'cannot be a perfect man, / Not being tried and tutor'd in the world' (I,iii,20–1). Both Valentine and Proteus thus depart Verona for Milan to gain broadening experience, to test friendship and love, to find adventure – in short, to learn.

As has often been pointed out, the plot of *The Two Gentlemen of Verona* is in some details like John Lyly's *Euphues* (1578), another story of friendship betrayed then reconciled.[63] In Lyly's romance, Euphues travels not from Verona to Milan but from Athens to Naples, described as 'a place of more pleasure than profite, and yet of more profite than pietie'.[64] Euphues meets Philautus there, and enters into a 'league of friendship'.[65] Despite this bond, however, he falls in love with Philautus' lady, much as Proteus falls in love with Silvia in Shakespeare's play. Like Proteus, too, Euphues betrays his pledge of friendship: 'Shall I not hazard my lyfe to obtain my love? . . . Yes *Euphues*, where love beareth sway, friendship can have no shew.'[66] Proteus rationalizes with regard to women, 'The law of friendship' (III,i,5) is nothing: 'In love / Who respects friend?' (V,iv,53–4). Philautus' discovery of Euphues' betrayal parallels Valentine's of Proteus', but eventually both sets of friends are reconciled at the end of their stories. Lyly's settings of Athens and Naples suggest a journey from the civilized world to a dangerous place, much as Shakespeare's Verona and Milan imply a movement from a protected home environment to a licensed and sophisticated city. In both cases though, an Italian place is where friendship is betrayed and actions are often questionable.

Most editors view Speed's greeting of Launce to 'Padua' and not 'Milan' at II,v,1 in the Folio as one of Shakespeare's many 'errors' in the play, possibly due to hasty writing or careless rewriting.[67] But surely this welcome is meant to be a joke by the quick-witted servant at the expense of the slow-witted one – Padua is, after all, in the opposite direction from Milan when travelling from Verona. Other slips, however, such as the substitution of 'Verona' for 'Milan' at V,iv,129 in the Folio, are not so easy to explain. There also seems to be some confusion in the play about whether the Duke of Milan is more than a duke. Thomas points out that at various times historically emperors did rule Milan.[68] The mistaken references to 'Emperor' rather than 'Duke' are perhaps understandable in that they all come from provincial Veronese. Panthino is one such, as is Antonio, who perhaps has not travelled in his youth and is thus anxious for his son to do so. Launce, too, errs by calling the Duke the

Emperor, but, to the dull servant, the duchy of Milan may have been as impressive as an empire or kingdom. Thomas writes: 'though in name (being but a duchy) it should not seem great, yet in very deed, both for the wealth of the country and for the quantity, the thing hath been of as great reputation as some realms of Europe. Out of doubt there have been some Dukes of Milan much greater in territory, wealthier in revenues and treasure, more puissant in wars, and finally, more honorable in peace than divers of them that had kingly titles'.[69] Antonio's reference to the 'Emperor's court' (I,iii,38) or Launce's to 'the Imperial's court' (II,iii,5) are imprecise but rather in character.

As is typical of the Italian plays, Shakespeare does not mention the cathedral of Milan or other important architectural features of his Milanese setting in *The Two Gentlemen of Verona*. Surprisingly, though, he does refer to 'Saint Gregory's Well' (IV,ii,84), an actual well near Milan that he may have seen pictured in Georg Braun's *Civitates Orbis Terrarum* (1572) or have found in a now lost source.[70] Beyond this remarkably precise detail, only 'gates' are mentioned as belonging to the city. The northern *Porta Nuova* of Milan, still standing today, is perhaps the 'North-gate' in the play (see III,i,260, 373) – but then any walled city would have a north gate. Shakespeare makes the way from Milan to Mantua mountainous (V,ii,46–7) not flat as it actually is. Further, Milan is imagined a seaport (see I,i,54; II,iii,35–6) rather than a river city, and connected to Verona primarily by water appropriate for 'ships'. Verona seems on a tidal river, much like, say, the Thames in London. 'So in *The Two Gentlemen of Verona*', we might conclude with H. B. Charlton, 'the scene is laid in . . . an Italy of romance not of physiographic authenticity'.[71]

A number of English details are to be discovered in the play. The names *Launce* and *Speed* are taken from English words. The customs of begging for soul-cakes at Hallowmas (II,i,25–6) is English, as are the Whitsuntide pageants (IV,iv,158–9), alehouses (II,v,54, 58), and 'lac'd mutton' (I,i,97). And, of course, Robin Hood.

There are Italianate details as well. The clowns come from the *Commedia dell'arte* tradition. Proteus' betrayal to the Duke of his friend's intended elopement, and request to keep this betrayal a secret from Valentine, seems decidedly Machiavellian. Ironically, the Duke thinks Valentine the Machiavel – a 'base intruder, overweening slave' (III,i,157) – for wooing Silvia, so much above him in station. Moryson reports that Italian fathers kept 'virgins . . .

locked up at home'.[72] The Duke nightly houses Silvia 'in an upper tow'r' and holds the key (III,i,35–6), even before he discovers her elopement plans. After he does, she is put in 'close prison' (III,i,237), and will be forced to marry Thurio. When Valentine informs the outlaws that he has been banished for killing a man, they are incredulous that so severe a punishment would attend 'so small a fault' (IV,i,31). The Second Outlaw, confirming proverbial Italian temperament, reports that he has killed a gentlemen 'in my mood' (IV,i,49). Murder in Italy was, by reputation, commonplace. There is music in the play, and there are sonnets too.

Shakespeare again has a learning motif in *The Two Gentlemen of Verona*. Though not Padua, Milan is still a place to learn. The play opens with an academic sounding disputation on the subject of love. Later, Launce uses the rhetoric of debate to argue a point with Speed (III,i,359–63). Crab disgraces his master when tested, and Launce has 'taught him, even as one would say precisely, "Thus would I teach a dog"' (IV,iv,5–6). Speed observes, in similarly relevant language, that Silvia manages Valentine completely: 'she hath taught her suitor, / He being her pupil, to become her tutor' (II,i,137–8). Julia would have Lucetta 'lesson' her on how she might journey to Proteus honourably (II,vii,5–7). Early in the play, and still in love with Julia, Proteus exclaims: 'Thou, Julia, thou hast metamorphis'd me, / Made me neglect my studies' (I,i,66–7).

Studies neglected, Proteus (whose name suggests the mythic character associated with change) first loves Julia, then changes the object of his passion to his friend's love Silvia: 'Even as one heat another heat expels, / Or as one nail by strength drives out another, / So the remembrance of my former love / Is by a new object quite forgotten' (II,iv,192–5). Shakespeare's image of the nails as a metaphor for a new mistress replacing an old one he found in Brooke's *Romeus and Juliet* ('as out of a planke a nayle a nayle doth drive, / So novell love out of the minde the auncient love doth rive' [ll. 207–8]), but Moryson uses it as well to describe the male Italian pursuit of courtesans, 'so driving out love with love, as one nayle with another'.[73] Ironically, the Duke considers Proteus constant in his affection for Julia, 'Love's firm votary' (III,ii,58–9). False Proteus, however, has betrayed his friend, and is seen willing to go to any length, even rape, to possess his newer passion Silvia. He has ceased to be a 'gentleman' from Verona, though his precipitous conversion at the end of the play is meant to redeem him at the last.

The other 'gentleman' from Verona, Valentine (whose name

suggests a lover) changes, too, during the course of the action. After Valentine has fallen in love with Silvia, Speed remarks: 'you are metamorphis'd with a mistress, that when I look on you, I can hardly think you are my master' (II,i,30–2). Valentine confesses his old 'life is alter'd now' (II,iv,128) because he has fallen in love.

Constant in her love for Proteus, Julia changes into Sebastian to pursue him. Protected by a disguise, she describes her former self to Silvia:

> She hath been fairer, madam, than she is:
> When she did think my master lov'd her well,
> She, in my judgment, was as fair as you;
> But since she did neglect her looking-glass,
> And threw her sun-expelling mask away,
> The air has starv'd the roses in her cheeks,
> And pinch'd the lily-tincture of her face,
> That now she is become as black as I.
>
> (IV,iv,149–56)

Sir Eglamour is metamorphosed from one of Julia's suitors (see I,ii,9) to a gentleman aiding Silvia's escape from her father's court (see IV,iii; V,i and ii), to a coward who runs from trouble (V,iii,6–7). Sir Thurio is a 'chameleon' who changes 'colour' (II,iv,23–4); he is transmogrified 'from a gentleman to a fool' (V,ii,24). The outlaws are 'reformed' (V,iv,156) in the forest, and are pardoned by a Duke who also has been converted by the green world (V,iv,158).

The exchange between Julia and Proteus near the end of the play sums up the moral concerning change and constancy in *The Two Gentlemen of Verona*. When Julia excuses her disguise with the lines, 'It is the lesser blot, modesty finds, / Women to change their shapes than men their minds' (V,iv,108–9), the newly forgiven and reformed Proteus agrees: "'tis true. O heaven, were man/But constant, he were perfect; that one error/Fills him with faults; makes him run through all th' sins:/Inconstancy falls off ere it begins. / What is in Silvia's face, but I may spy / More fresh in Julia's with a constant eye?' (V,iv,109–15). Proteus has learned his lesson. Travel and love breed change and learning in Shakespeare's Italian scene.

4
Beyond the Signory

After the Venetian Signory, the second Italian centre of interest for Renaissance England was Tuscany.[1] This region was reputed especially beautiful in a physical sense. The purest and best Italian was supposedly spoken here.[2] Florence was the area's political and commercial locus, a city connected with Machiavelli in the English mind. Chapman's *All Fools*, for instance, set in Florence, has the comic 'knight' Gostanzo, 'a Machiavel, / A miserable politician' (II,i,201–2). In Webster's *The White Devil*, the Duke of Florence's actions are 'the rare tricks of a Machiavillain' (V,iii,195). Of course, Machiavellians can be found everywhere in Renaissance drama, but Florence was their appropriate setting.

William Thomas' sole source for his history of Florence, in his more general history of Italy, was Machiavelli. Thomas describes him as 'a notable learned man and secretary of late days to the commonwealth there'.[3] Thomas thought Florence 'an excellent fair city', remarking, among other things, the 'many fair palaces and sumptuous houses', 'four very fair bridges', and the Duomo and campanile of Giotto.[4] He reports that the city walls are constructed 'with square stone in manner as hard as flint and of a great height, with a number of goodly towers after the ancient building, strong enough to defend but nothing apt for artillery to offend after the manner of these days, for they were builded before the invention of guns'.[5]

All of Italy, but Florence in particular, was associated with warfare and its latest weaponry and technology. Dante fought for Florence against Arezzo in the Battle of Campaldino in 1289. During the Renaissance, the Florentine Guelphs supported the Pope against the Sienese Ghibellines, the Emperor's allies, for the remnants of the Holy Roman Empire. Indeed, as long as most could remember, there had been almost constant bloody warfare between Florence and Siena in the Chianti region. Machiavelli's *The Art of War*, published in 1520, was the first of his works translated into English (1550), and it was considered for a time a definitive text on its subject for English soldiers. Other contemporary books in this Florentine tradition included Nanni's *Oratini Militari* (1560), Bocchi's *Discorso* (1580), Carafa's *Libre tre* (1581), and Bacci's *Trattato* (1601). Officers and foot soldiers from Italy manned the armies of many European states. Petruccio Ubaldini and one Captain Tiberio, for example, fought with the forces of Henry VIII and Edward VI.[6] Moryson writes that the Duke of Florence supplemented his own troops with mercenaries from other Italian cities: he offered 'large yearely stipends even in tyme of peace, to forraine Princes and noblemen (I meane Italians but not under his Dominion) . . . that he might ingage them to his service in tyme of warr'.[7] Though Bertram is not Italian, the Duke of Florence in *All's Well That Ends Well* gives him a responsible command in the city's army.

Beyond Tuscany and Florence for the English was the ever more dangerous and mythical south of Italy. According to Mario Praz, the Messina of *Much Ado About Nothing* 'is clearly an imaginary town'.[8] Even for a widely travelled person of Shakespeare's time, Sicilian Messina was off the beaten track; the people who found it were on their way to Malta or perhaps returning from the Levant. George Sandys was one such, and he notes the city as first to insure banks and guarantee safe deposits.[9] The 'nineteene yeares' traveller William Lithgow met very few fellow Britishers there.[10]

Shakespeare is historically accurate in designating the House of Aragon rulers of Sicily, for this Spanish family assumed control of the island after the Vespers Insurrection at Palermo (1283) when the French were driven out. A 'Prince of Arragon', we recall, figures as one of Portia's unsuccessful suitors in *The Merchant of Venice*; this presumed Catholic chooses the silver casket and finds in it a 'portrait of a blinking idiot' (II,ix,54). In Webster's *The White Devil*, the 'Cardinal of Arragon' announces the election of the new Pope. But Shakespeare's *Much Ado About Nothing* avoids directly confronting Aragon's and Spain's religion. Don Pedro is treated sympathetically. Though the ruling prince, he is also a genial friend and father figure. Leonato appears to be his native governor. The Italians in the play are addressed as 'Signoir', while the Spanish prince and his brother are 'Dons'.[11] Dogberry, of course, gets it all wrong: 'we are the poor Duke's officers' (III,v,19–20) – no duke is mentioned anywhere.

After Sicily and Messina what? The island football punted to a beyond further away in space and imagination than any geographical Italy or even Illyria. But home, too – after all, an island.

And there is yet one last literal Italian setting alluded to in *The Tempest*. Alonso is King of Naples.

The region of Naples had important classical as well as modern associations for the Renaissance English. With its geological peculiarities and volcanic activity, it was then as now an exotic landscape. The ancients regarded Lago d'Averno as the entrance to the Underworld, and Lake Campania, along the Bay of Naples, was remembered as where Ulysses narrowly escaped the sirens. Naples is 'sometimes called Parthenope', reminds Thomas, a reference to the legend that the city sprung up around the siren Parthenope's tomb.[12] Ascham saw all of Italy as 'Circes Court', and Lyly's *Euphues*, set in Naples, also uses a siren image to indicate the temptations of the place.[13] Most descriptions of Naples in Lyly's romance are negative. At first Euphues will not believe an old native 'that *Naples* is a canckered storehouse of all strife, a common stewes for all strumpettes, the sinke of shame, and the very nurse of all sin', but later, with first-hand experience, he admits the city is 'the nourisher of wantonnesse', 'the most cursed towne in all *Italy*'.[14]

Throughout the Renaissance, Naples was in constant political turmoil. A kingdom of sorts, it was fought over by France and Spain with the Pope looking on. Duke Ludovico Sforza of Milan had invited Charles VIII and France to invade Italy and claim Naples; this action brought in competing Spanish armies. The treaty of Granada (1500) gave a share of Naples to Spain, and three years later they took the entire realm as a 'province'. In Shakespeare's day, Naples like Milan belongs to Spain. Moryson observes that the Neapolitans 'hate the french their old lordes, and no lesse the Spainardes who presently governe them'; he notes 'the Neapolitan language is most corrupted with the Spanish'.[15]

Yet the Spanish viceroy and his court at Naples were recognized as a highly aristocratic society. Thomas found it 'very princely', formerly even 'greater than that of Milan for train of gentlemen', though perhaps now on a par.[16] The Anglo-Spanish treaty of 1604 opened Naples and Milan to the English, and excited renewed interest in these places. Perhaps Shakespeare was capitalizing on this interest in *The Tempest*.

But, then again, Naples always held a special attraction for the Renaissance English. It elicited a kind of 'fascination of the abomination'. Thomas blamed the constant political turmoil on its native citizens: 'since the decay of the Roman Empire no realm in all the world hath been so much subject to alterations and wars, principally through occation of the inhabitants themselves, who were always divided in partakings to their own confusion'.[17] The Neapolitan character was thoroughly suspect. Though Thomas was well entertained in the city, he reports that 'most men' think the Neapolitan 'to be a great flatterer and full of craft'; indeed, 'the Neapolitans are scarcely trusted on their words . . . because [of] the wonted general ill opinion of their unsteadfastness'.[18] Nashe writes, by way of Jack Wilton, 'The *Neapolitane* carrieth the bloodieth mind, and is the most secret fleering murderer: whereuponn it is growen to a common proverbe, *Ile give him the Neapolitan shrug*, when one intends to play the villaine and make no boast of it.'[19] In Marlowe's *Edward II*, the murderer Lightborn

> . . . learn'd in Naples how to poison flowers,
> To strangle with a lawn thrust through the throat
> To pierce the windpipe with a needle's point,
> Or whilst one is asleep, to take a quill
> And blow a little powder in his ears,
> Or open his mouth and pour quicksilver down.
>
> (V,iv,31–6)

Naples also had the worst reputation for highway robbery. Thomas contends that 'almost no stranger can travel the realm unrobbed, specially between Rome and Naples'.[20] Syphilis, too, was associated with Naples, and commonly called the 'Neapolitan disease'. In *Troilus and Cressida*, Thersites refers to 'the Neapolitan bone-ache' (II,iii,18–19), and in *Othello* the nasal sound of the musicians' instruments causes the clown to ask if they have 'been in Naples' (III,i,3–4) – that is, have they been affected by venereal disease. Moryson writes that 60 000 'harlots . . . were sayd to be in the Citty of Naples'.[21]

On the positive side, Naples was known for its breed of fine horses, 'vulgarly called Corsers of their swiftness'.[22] In *The Merchant of Venice*, Portia ridicules her Neapolitan suitor's love of horses: she describes him as 'a colt indeed, for he doth nothing but talk of his horse, and he makes it a great appropriation to his own good parts that he can shoe him himself. I am much afeard . . . his mother play'd false with a smith' (I,ii,40–4). John Florio's *Second Frutes*, among other works by Italians, pokes fun at English riding customs, and perhaps here Shakespeare wished to poke back his own fun. As with Milan, Naples is not a literal setting in *The Tempest*. Rather, it provides a backdrop for the action on Shakespeare's unnamed island. The spotted and fabulous reputation of Naples, however, reinforces the dangerous and magical atmosphere of Prospero's land, and lends credibility to the unsavory characters of King Alonso and his brother Sebastian.

Shakespeare's settings beyond the Venetian Signory are taken up in part with a familiar theme found in the *terra firma* plays. Travel may be from France to Florence rather than from one Italian city to another in *All's Well That Ends Well*, but the education theme is still dominant. As does Bertram in his play, Claudio, Benedick, and Beatrice learn important lessons in their play. And, in *The Tempest*, Frank Kermode notes, 'learning is a major theme'.[23] When Sebastian exacerbates Alonso's grief by reminding him of it, Gonzalo instructs the King's brother: 'My Lord Sebastian,/The truth you speak doth lack some gentleness, / And time to speak it in. You rub the sore, / When you should bring the plaster' (II,i,137–40). The dominant teacher in *The Tempest* though is obviously Prospero, who instructs from the beginning to the end of the action on the island.

He is first viewed informing Miranda about their past. Like a conscientious instructor during the history, he is very aware of his audience. At various points in his narrative, he asks if she is listening: 'Dost thou attend me?' (I,ii,78); 'Thou attend'st not!' (I,ii,87); 'Dost thou hear?' (I,ii,106). Prospero describes how he lost his dukedom because of commitment not to government but to 'the liberal arts, / . . . those being all my study' (I,ii,73–4). He confesses that he had 'dedicated [himself] / To closeness and the bettering of my mind' (I,ii,89–90); 'my library / Was dukedom large enough' (I,ii,109–10). When he is banished, he recounts that Gonzalo 'Knowing I lov'd my books, he furnish'd me / From mine own library with volumes that / I prize above my dukedom' (I,ii,166–8). Caliban acknowledges the importance of Prospero's books on the island. They are the source of his magical powers. In the monster's words, 'without them / He's but a sot, as I am' (III,ii,92–3). Prospero has been a careful 'schoolmaster' to his daughter. He has made Miranda 'more profit / Than other princess' can, that have more time / For vainer hours, and tutors not so careful' (I,ii,172–4).

Prospero tries in vain to make Caliban humane but the lessons will not take. He has taught the monster 'how / To name the bigger light, and how the less' (I,ii,334–5). Miranda, too, has tried to teach him 'each hour/One thing or other' (I,ii,354–5) – most especially 'language' (I,ii,363–4). Stephano teaches him how to 'troll the catch' (III,ii,117). But Caliban uses language to 'curse' (I,ii,364) and his other lessons do not leave 'any print of goodness' (I,ii,352). Prospero ultimately sees Caliban 'A devil, a born devil, on whose nature/Nurture can never stick; on whom my pains,/Humanely taken, all lost, quite lost;/And as with age his body uglier grows,/So his mind cankers' (IV,i,188–92).

Miranda learns about love at first sight when she meets Ferdinand, but her father is initially harsh to her new friend. Miranda intervenes by instructing Prospero: 'He's gentle, and not fearful' (I,ii,469). The magician responds ironically: 'My foot [i.e., inferior] my tutor?' (I,ii,470). He will make Ferdinand labour to win Miranda so that the prince will prize her the more; indeed, Prospero makes Ferdinand carry logs, Caliban's work.

Antonio would 'teach' Sebastian how to seize the crown of Naples (II,i,222). Prospero's banquet is a device meant to instruct Antonio, Sebastian, and Alonso, the 'three men of sin' (III,iii,53), of the wrong done to the exiled duke. The wedding masque is another lesson, this one reminding all of the inevitable cycle of nature and life. Prospero's speech at the end of the masque drives home the point that existence is mysterious and magical: 'We are such stuff/As dreams are made on; and our little life/Is rounded with a sleep' (IV,i,156–8). Thus, according to Prospero, most unItalianate here but most Christian, 'The rarer action is/In virtue than in vengeance' (V,i,27–8). All is forgiven in the end – the final lesson.

Shakespeare's Italian settings beyond the Venetian *terra firma* are Florence, Messina, and an unnamed island. Florence is handled in a vague but credible way in terms of its history and reputation, while Messina is harder to pin down as geographical Italy. The island in *The Tempest* teases us to allegory.

A ALL'S WELL THAT ENDS WELL

Shakespeare sets nine scenes of *All's Well That Ends Well* (in Acts III and IV) in or about Florence. However, nothing of its geographical location, natural beauty, or physical characteristics are remarked; there is no Arno, Cathedral, or Bell Tower alluded to. Moreover, the Florentines in his play do not seem distinctively Florentine. The

Duke is never mentioned as a Medici, and the old Widow and Diana's family name is 'Capilet', a name associated with another city, as we know from *Romeo and Juliet*. Thomas' observations that Florentine maidens are kept 'so strait that in manner no stranger may see them'[24] does not jibe with Shakespeare's Diana out on the street watching the soldiers come home (III,v). On the other hand, Shakespeare does seem to know that Siena was a traditional enemy of Florence, and that France was at times an ally. Moryson notes that France and Spain jockeyed continually for regional influence in Tuscany, and just as he was writing his *Itinerary* 'the Duke of Florence had great strength by Catherine de Medici, then Queene of France'.[25] Siena was, in fact, under Florence's control by Shakespeare's time.

Florentine natives supposedly were very garrulous, and they had a great reputation for conversation.[26] It is as if Shakespeare created his Frenchman Parolles with this Florentine trait in mind. Parolles is most of all verbal. His stories, though perhaps nothing but lies (III,vi,9–10), nonetheless abound. After the Clown pokes fun at the faddish phrase 'O Lord, Sir!' (II,ii,41–62), Parolles uses similar fashionable retorts and interjections in the scene that follows (see II,iii,11–40). Thus Parolles' slang is seen as up-to-date. He is described also as a 'manifold linguist' (IV,iii,236) who 'hath a smack of all . . . languages' (IV,i,15–16), Italian among them (IV,i,71–3). A few times during the course of the play he comes out with *'coraggio'* (II,v,92) and *'capriccio'* (II,iii,293). The name *Parolles*, to be sure, means 'words' in French (see V,ii,39–40).

Parolles' banter with Helena on the subject of virginity (I,i,110–65) seems a parody of the language of the war manuals associated with Florence. Machiavelli's *The Art of War*, for example, contains both dialogue and a section on the use of mines for blowing up cities.[27] Helena's witty defence of chastity in the face of Parolles' attack shows them both to be studied soldiers with different battlefields in mind.

Parolles' talkativeness about the lost drum which he promises to recover parallels an episode in Nashe's *The Unfortunate Traveller*, another work with a partly Italian setting.[28] The source for the main plot of *All's Well That Ends Well* is derived ultimately from Boccaccio's *Decameron*, the ninth novel of the third day.[29] The names in Shakespeare's play, however, suggest a French intermediary, and William Painter's version of the Italian story. In Painter there is no political alliance between France and Florence, and the Italian setting seems only a backdrop for romantic adventure. Shakespeare, on the other hand, makes Florence a training ground in warfare for French youth, which indeed it was at times. There are few Italian details in the play claiming attention. 'St. Francis' does seem an apt Inn sign for Florence, honouring as it does the renowned Tuscan saint. 'Antonio' and 'Escalus' are similarly appropriate names for Italian soldiers (III,v,76–7), as are 'Captain Spurio' (II,i,42–3) and others in the cosmopolitan Florentine army (see IV,iii,160–6).

From one point of view, *All's Well That Ends Well* is similar to *The Taming of the Shrew*. If the latter tells the story of Petruchio taming Kate, the former is about Helena's taming of Bertram. Helena's father, as Petruchio's, has recently died, and Helena uses her wits, as does Petruchio, to improve her lot. 'Wealthily' for Helena, however, is not so much a matter of material riches, as a matter of love and movement up the social ladder. She acknowledges Bertram to be 'so above me', that there is 'ambition in my love' (I,i,87,90).

Both *The Taming of the Shrew* and *All's Well That Ends Well* detail strange weddings and their aftermaths. In both plays, marriage is just the beginning of the taming process. If Petruchio must bridle an almost irrepressible Kate when he marries her, so too must Helena tame a Bertram who sets for his new wife impossible conditions for the consummation of their marriage. But both tamers are equal to their tasks. Perhaps in keeping with traditional womanly decorum, Helena is more modest and covert in pursuit of Bertram's reformation than is Petruchio with Kate – he seems the stereotypical dominating male. But method aside, the social poseurs Kate and Bertram are each effectively shown their true selves as against their immature posturing. Both ultimately kiss their spouses, after having refused them kisses earlier on.

All's Well That Ends Well is in large part Bertram's story, the story of the education of a young gentleman. Like Lucentio in *The Taming of the Shrew*, Bertram is an innocent abroad – removed from his provincial home. Again the English allegory is easy to see. As with many young Englishmen, Bertram's learning involves the experience of travel. In Bertram's case, he moves first from his native Rossillion to the sophisticated court at Paris and, ultimately, to dangerous Italy and the Florentine wars. The play opens with the wise counsellor LaFew telling the fatherless Bertram that he 'shall find of the King . . . a father' (I,i,6–7). The Countess sends her son off to court with a plea to LaFew who will accompany him: '"Tis an unseason'd courtier, good my lord, / Advise him' (I,i,71–2). Helena, too, is worried about Bertram. She knows that the court is 'a learning place', and that Bertram is under the bad influence of Parolles, 'a notorious liar' (I,i,100). Indeed, Parolles is soon seen instructing Bertram as to his social behaviour: 'Use a more spacious ceremony to the noble lords', he says, 'Be more expressive to them' (II,i,50–2). Caught between those who care for him from home and his bad advisor teaching him deceit and social posturing, Bertram's position suggests a sort of Faust situation.

At the court, the French King is sending volunteers to the Florentine wars. One Lord suggests that this action has Machiavellian purpose: 'It well may serve / A nursery to our gentry' (I,ii,15–16); that is, it will train French soldiers for our own causes. The King, however, has prophetic warnings for his young countrymen: 'see that you come / Not to woo honor, but to wed it' (II,i,14–15), and, in a similar vein, 'Those girls of Italy, take heed of them' (II,i,19). Whether for French youth or English youth, Italy presented dangerous moral temptations. The King's fears turn out to be apt forewarnings for Bertram, though he is told that presently he is 'Too young' to go off to these wars, ''tis too early' for him now, and he must wait until 'the next year' (II,i,28). But following the counsel of his bad teacher Parolles, Bertram disobeys the King's explicit commandment, and 'steal[s] away' to the wars. By doing so, Bertram compromises the notion of duty and obedience upon which his old world hierarchical code of honour and nobility is based. One pays homage to one's king. Throughout this episode, Shakespeare stresses Bertram's youth and the upstart Parolles' negative influence.

Helena follows Bertram to Paris, and by effecting the King's cure gets to choose him for a husband. 'This is the man' (II,iii,104), she says; but Helena is wrong to think that Bertram is really a 'man' yet. He is sorely lacking both in experience and education. His immaturity is underlined when he disobeys the King a second time by refusing the humbly born Helena for a wife. 'Proud, scornful boy' (II,iii,151) the King exclaims, then threatens to cast Bertram from 'my care for ever / Into the staggers and the careless lapse / Of youth and ignorance' (II,iii,162–4). Seeming to relent, Bertram marries Helena. His plan, though, is to go off 'to the Tuscan wars, and never bed her' (II,iii,273). Like a willful adolescent, Bertram leaves for 'those Italian fields / Where noble fellows strike' (II,iii,290–1). But almost as Grace in pursuit of wayward Christian youth (say, Una chasing Red Cross Knight), Helena follows Bertram to Italy, a very symbol of temptation, to rescue him ultimately despite seemingly hopeless odds. In this connection, it is worth observing that Helena's namesake is a saint especially revered by the English Church because of her supposed British origin. St. Helena was thought to be, according to one legend, daughter of an ancient king – the 'Old King Cole' (Coelus, Earl of Colchester) of the nursery rhyme.[30] More familiarly, she was the Emperor Constantine's mother, who, like Shakespeare's Helena, was of lowly birth (her father was an innkeeper). This St. Helena also had husband troubles; she was repudiated by Constantine Chlorus in A.D. 292. There was much confusion among the English concerning Constantine the Great's mother and another more British St. Helena, also of the fourth century. This latter Helena had French and Italian connections, interesting for our play.[31] She was the daughter of a Welsh prince (Eudaf), whose son together with Helena's husband fought in Gaul and Italy. This St. Helena's son, Owen Finddu, is credited with achieving British independence in ancient times.

Despite LaFew's expressed suspicions that Parolles' character, like fashionable Italy, consists of nothing but veneer and ornament, Bertram continues to be directed by him. Bertram assures LaFew that Parolles 'is very great in knowledge' (II,v,8–9), but the counsellor knows better: 'there can be no kernel in this light nut; the soul of this man is his clothes. Trust him not in matters of heavy consequence' (II,v,43–5). Parolles may be intended as a symbol of the resplendent Roman religion. In any case, La Few's good advice goes unheeded, and, imitating his false teacher, Bertram lies to Helena when he leaves her suddenly immediately following their wedding.

Bertram's letter to his mother, detailing his treatment of Helena, is received with dismay by the Countess; she echoes the King's earlier rebuke by calling her son a 'rash and unbridled boy' (III,ii,28). Helena, she says, 'deserves a lord / That twenty such rude boys might tend upon, / And call her hourly mistress' (III,ii,81–3). Knowing that Parolles is the bad influence, she excuses Bertram somewhat: 'My son corrupts a well-derived nature / With his [Parolles'] inducement' (III,ii,88–9). Her message for Bertram is 'that his sword can never win / The honour that he loses' (III,ii,93–4) by his ignoble and juvenile behaviour.

Bertram does well in the Italian wars. He captures Siena's 'great'st commander, and . . . with his own hand he slew the Duke's brother' (III,v,5–7). Nevertheless, he continues to be a disciple of Parolles. Mariana warns Diana of them both (III,v,16–28), and the girl knows already about Parolles. With stereotypical Italianate fury, she claims that were she his wife, 'I would poison that vile rascal' (III,v,84).

The plot to unmask Parolles affords Bertram the opportunity for change from his immature self. 'Do you think I am so far deceiv'd in him?' (III,vi,6), Bertram asks the French lords. The answer is obvious: 'he's a most notable coward, [and] an infinite and endless liar' (III,vi,9–10). As LaFew had done before, the lords warn Bertram that Parolles 'might at some great and trusty business in a main danger fail you' (III,vi,14–16). They insist, 'You do not know him, my lord, as we do' (III,vi,90–1). But Bertram soon finds out about the real Parolles; he is uncovered as a 'counterfeit module' (IV,iii,99).

Since Bertram has been 'misled with a snipt-taffata fellow' (IV,v,1–2), La Few assures the Countess that all is not lost with her son. There is still hope for his reformation, and for him to live up to the model of his noble dead father. However, Bertram requires positive instruction in virtue and honour. Some of this is provided by Diana, ironically an Italian girl and the girl he would dishonour. After wittily fending off Bertram's seductive behaviour, she argues that 'yielding' in marriage is 'duty, such, my lord, / As you owe to your wife' (IV,ii,12–13). Diana's chaste talk goes with the suggestiveness of her name. But, at this point, Bertram will hear nothing sensible. Later, however, when he receives a letter from his mother, a lord reports that 'he chang'd almost into another man' (IV,iii,5). This diction suggests Bertram's ongoing learning and coming maturity. Indeed, Bertram returns to France from Florence physically changed. The Clown remarks the 'patch of velvet on's face. Whether there be a scar under't or no, the velvet knows, but 'tis a goodly patch of velvet. His left cheek is a cheek of two pile and a half, but his right cheek is worn bare' (IV,v,95–8). Here then is another outward sign of a different Bertram.

Her son home again to proper values in a supportive setting, the Countess pleads with the King to accept Bertram once again into the royal good graces, to forgive his fault: 'I beseech your Majesty to make it / Natural rebellion, done i'th'blade of youth' (V,iii,5–6). The King responds that he will reinstate Bertram, then adds some of his own lessons for the wayward youth (V,iii,57–66). But it is soon apparent that the young man still has in place some ingrained lessons learned in Italy. When Diana confronts him publicly, he dismisses her as a courtesan, 'a common gamester to the camp' (V,iii,188). It is not, however, until his lies about his family ring, the symbol of his old world honour, are uncovered that Bertram finally confesses all. He was, alas, willing to pawn his noble name and lineage for present gratification. In the end, presumably Shakespeare now wishes his audience to feel that Bertram has learned his lesson, and that his experience in Italy has shown him the way to maturity, virtue, and wisdom. The lesson for English youth is clear: Italy's fashionable temptations can compromise the most basic virtues and teachings of home.

In *The History of Italy*, Thomas writes of three things which characterize a gentleman: 'the first is arms, to maintain withal his honor; the second love, to show himself gentle and not cruel of nature; and the third is learning, to be able to know, to understand and to utter his opinion in matters of weight'.[32] Bertram's experience seems to be measured in these terms. He has distinguished himself in 'arms', but must 'show himself gentle and not cruel of nature' in love, and ultimately reflect his 'learning'. While there may be some debate concerning the ultimate tone of *All's Well That Ends Well*, it seems clear that whether or not Bertram has learned by the end of the action, the opportunity for the education of this young man is in part what has been centrally presented. Though of noble birth and great promise, Bertram requires the nurture of war, love, and learning to educate him to the wisdom necessary to compliment the fortune of his birth. Virtue growing out of experience is needed to ennoble him fully.

B   MUCH ADO ABOUT NOTHING

The Claudio and Hero plot of *Much Ado About Nothing* harkens back to Italian sources.[33] The fifth canto of Ariosto's *Orlando Furioso* (1516) in its English poetic elaboration by Peter Beverley (c. 1566) and/or rendering by Sir John Harington (1591) may have stimulated Shakespeare's retelling of the classic story of a lover betrayed into believing his mistress false. Shakespeare's most direct source, however, is thought to be Matteo Bandello's *La Prima de le Novelle* (1554), perhaps in François Belleforest's French version or in some English version now lost. Bandello seems to have been the origin for several of the names in Shakespeare's play, though Lionati to

Leonato is easier to see than Piero to Pedro. Shakespeare's Messina also takes its cue from Bandello, but, as we shall observe, there is another more special reason that the play is set in this seaport city. A. R. Humphreys, the New Arden editor, describes Messina as 'essentially good natured': 'it is a lively, sociable world presented through its etiquettes and enjoyments, . . . creating a close-knit scene for the cheerful manoeuvres of affluent leisure'.[34] He continues, 'it is a scene of social engagement, courtly diplomacies and festive pleasure, a cheerful world of carnival'.[35] A city of sophisticated foreigners, Messina entertains not only Spaniards but Italians from the north.

Claudio (whose name, by the way, is traditional for a *Commedia dell'arte* lover) is Florentine (I,i,11), and shares qualities of courtesy with his fellow native Cassio in *Othello*. Because his heartless repudiation of Hero is so overwhelming later in the play, one might forget that Claudio is modest, graceful, and sympathetic earlier on. Claudio is clearly young and inexperienced. He willingly puts the wooing of his lady into Don Pedro's hands, and is disappointed but resigned when he thinks the prince has won Hero for himself. The real truth discovered, he is so meek and retiring that he must be prompted to kiss his love. J. W. Draper finds Claudio's interest in Hero's dowry consistent with the Florentine reputation for financial shrewdness.[36] However, as we have noticed, most young suitors in Shakespeare's Italian plays, no matter where they are from, are interested in such matters.

Benedick is from the university city of Padua (I,i,35–6), and his wit and learning are everywhere in evidence.[37] He is obviously widely read. He alludes learnedly to 'Cupid' (I,i,254), 'Leander' (V,ii,30), and 'Troilus' (V,ii,31). His reasoning is wittily balanced, as in his soliloquy at the start of II,iii (7–36). He knows foreign languages – 'he hath the tongues' (V,i,166) – and not, one suspects, just a word or two of them like Sir Andrew Aguecheek. Moreover, Benedick is still the student open to new information and to change. With characteristic but comic logic he declares: 'the world must be peopled. When I said I would die a bachelor, I did not think I should live till I were married' (II,iii,242–4). He acknowledges his transformation: 'Gallants, I am not as I have been' (III,ii,15).

Yet despite their stated places of origin, Claudio and Benedick seem as much English as specifically Italian young men. The courtesy of Claudio and the wit of Benedick are characteristic of many a nubile romantic hero, no matter where he is from. There are also a number of clearly English touches in the play: references to 'a Scotch jig' (II,i,74, 75), the 'Hundred Merry Tales' jest book (II,i,130), the song 'Light a' love' (III,iv,44), and 'swords' and 'bucklers' (V,ii,17–18). Messina would have wine cellars not the alluded to 'alehouses' (III,iii,42) as in Shakespeare's play. Margaret and Ursula, 'Meg' (III,iv,8, 98) and 'Ursley' (III,i,4), have English sounding names. Dogberry and his watch, 'Verges', 'Oatcake', and 'Sea-coal', are certainly English types with English names, despite Dogberry's *palabras* (III,iv,16) and other 'fine' words.

Messina in *Much Ado About Nothing* has no specific geographical details of place, but there are some light touches in the play that evoke a vaguely Italian atmosphere. When inspired to poetry Benedick and Beatrice are prone to the sonnet form (see III,i,107–16; V,iv,87), Leonato has a family tomb like the Capulets in *Romeo and Juliet*, and Beatrice refers to Benedick as 'Signior Mountanto' (I,i,30) – using an Italian fencing term. Venice is mentioned as a place associated with love (I,i,271–2). In the manner of the stereotypical Italian spy in a drama of palace intrigue, Borachio 'whipt me behind the arras' (I,iii,60–1). (The baitings of Beatrice and Benedick, and the watch's fortunate overhearing of Don John's plot against Hero are other examples of the play's prominent eavesdropping motif.) 'Would the cook were a' my mind!' (I,iii,72–3), exclaims Don John, who wishes to poison more than good humour. Specific references to 'poison' are to be found at II,ii,21 and V,i,246.

There are two sides to the Italian character revealed in *Much Ado About Nothing*. First of all, there is the volatile 'temperament' demonstrated by the emotionally wounded Claudio; he lashes out extravagantly against the innocent Hero. A recent editor of *The Prince* describes Machiavelli's character in terms precisely appropriate to Claudio: 'Like a great many Tuscans, he had a horror of being taken for a dupe, and to avoid that appearance did not mind sometimes being considered a monster.'[38] Beatrice's command to 'Kill Claudio' as a way for Benedick to prove his love is another example of what the English considered stereotypical Italian temperament.

The other side of the Italian coin is the courtliness of the wit, friendship, and most actions of the central characters. Castiglione's *Il Cortegiano* may well have provided the model for the wit combats of Beatrice and Benedick in the exchanges between Lady Emilia and Lord Gaspare Pallavicino, and have also suggested the genteel behaviour of the aristocratic characters in Shakespeare's play.[39]

Barbara Lewalski has noticed that the phrase 'much ado' recurs in Book IV of Sir Thomas Hoby's translation.[40] 'Balthazar', the name the playwright gives to Don Pedro's musical attendant, was, of course, Castiglione's Christian name *Baldassare*; it was a name associated with courtesy in the Renaissance.[41]

Italy, and to a lesser extent Spain and France, set the English fashion for Shakespeare's age. A Venetian ambassador to England, Jacopo Soranzo, noted in correspondence that English styles copied the Italian.[42] Portia remarks on the strangeness of clothing of her English wooer Falconbridge: 'How oddly he is suited! I think he bought his doublet in Italy, his round hose in France, his bonnet in Germany, and his behavior every where' (I,ii,73–6). In Marlowe's *Edward II*, Gaveston 'wears a short Italian hooded cloak, / Larded with pearl, and in his Tuscan cap / A jewel of more value than the crown' (I,iv,415–17). When 'contrary to . . . Italian fashion [Webster's Duchess of Malfi] wears a loose-bodied gown' (II,i,78), she is suspected of being pregnant. Thomas seems awed by Italian fashion: 'the gentlewomen generally for gorgeous attire, apparel, and jewells exceed, I think, all other women of our known world'.[43]

Fashion is a key word in *Much Ado About Nothing*. Borachio plays with it in a number of lines as he describes his wooing of Margaret as Hero to his friend Conrade (III,iii,118, 121, 122, 124, 139, 141, 143). His point is that clothes can deceive. Benedick finds the love-smitten Claudio lying 'ten nights awake carving the fashion of a new doublet' (II,iii,17–18). There is a reference to 'the Duchess of Milan's gown' (III,iv,15–16), and to the 'rebato' (III,iv,6) ruff. After Hero's repudiation, Antonio challenges Claudio and Don Pedro calling them 'fashion-monging boys, / That lie and cog and flout, deprave and slander, / Go anticly, and show outward hideousness' (V,i,94–6). Early in the play, Beatrice wishes to know Benedick's current friend, since 'He wears his faith but as the fashion of his hat' (I,i,75–6). Leonato will disdain 'the fashion of the world . . . to avoid cost' (I,i,97–8), and entertain Don Pedro and his friends in an extravagant manner.

Much Ado About Nothing is Shakespeare's only play set in Messina, and the question may be asked why here of all places. Any number of other locales might have served the playwright for his *après*-war gathering of courtship and deceit. Why this one specifically? There seems some buried allusion to be discovered in the play.

In Shakespeare's day, Messina had quite specific associations for the Christian west. It was the launching point for the last galleys war in naval history. The Battle of Lepanto, fought on 7 October 1571, some twenty-seven or so years before *Much Ado About Nothing*, resulted in a great Christian victory against the Ottoman Empire.[44]

Pope Pius V had managed somehow to get Spain and Venice, among others, to cooperate with him and form a 'Holy League' alliance for waging war against Islam – the Turks and their allies. Don John of Austria, the 'bastard' brother of Philip II of Spain, was the Captain General of the Holy League fleet. Thus, there is an association of setting, character name, and Don John's circumstances of birth recalled in Shakespeare's play.

The Christian victory at Lepanto is historically noteworthy not only as the last great galley action in the history of naval warfare, but also for putting to rest the western notion of Turkish invincibility. Lepanto was the battle in which Cervantes (born the same year as Shakespeare) lost the use of his left hand. Ultimately, however, Lepanto turned out to be 'much ado about nothing': the victory was never followed up by the Christians. Pius V's death and the Holy League's continual bickering about selfish interests saw to that. As one scholar writes: 'It is generally considered that the battle of Lepanto was one of the great turning points of history, but modern historians have been hard pressed to explain why. Militarily the Holy League derived little immediate advantage from the victory. No territory changed hands in the wake of the battle. . . . It is apparent that in the short-term military sense Lepanto accomplished little or nothing.'[45]

But for the late sixteenth and early seventeenth centuries, Lepanto fired the Christian imagination. To commemorate the wonderful victory, 7 October was declared a perpetual holiday throughout most of Europe. On the heels of the Ottoman defeat celebrations abounded, with a special one at Messina to honour Don John's return to the city. A statue by Andrea Calamech was erected there as a memorial to the great general. Many songs, poems, and paintings were offered throughout the Christian world. Among these were a number of English works. George Gascoigne devoted part of his 1572 wedding masque, in honour of the English Montague's weddings, to Lepanto.[46] Abraham Holland wrote *Naumachia. or, A Poeticall Description of the cruell and bloudie Sea-fight or Battaile of Lepanto*.[47] The 'Epistle to the Reader', included with the revision of this work (1626; STC 13579), details Queen Elizabeth's response to news of the victory: 'Shee commanded the Citizens of *London*, to give Almightie GOD humble and heartie thankes, Her

Sacred selfe performing the same: The *Londoners* also made Bonfires, and showed other pleasant signes of rejoycing.' In 1576, the future James VI of Scotland, who would become Shakespeare's James I, published his poem about the great victory.[48] The 'Authors Preface to the Reader' indicates that James was about twelve or thirteen when he penned his more than 1100 lines (including epilogue choruses). In *Lepanto* he writes of 'Messena', where the Christian armies convened, and 'There Don Ioan d'Austria came, / Their Generall great . . .' (l. 205).

But why then, if all Christendom was singing in praise of Don John – indeed, if the present Queen and future King of England joined the chorus – would Shakespeare have created such a villainous namesake in his *Much Ado About Nothing*? To find reasons, we must consider the historical Don John's relations with England.

First and foremost, Don John was a prominent Catholic, stepbrother to Philip II who was the Spanish King and muscular military arm of the Roman religion. Philip, we recall, had married the English Catholic Queen Mary I in 1554 (his father, the Emperor Charles V, gave him Milan and Naples as a wedding present). When Mary died in 1558, Philip offered his hand to Elizabeth but was refused. Following this, as we might imagine, Elizabeth's queenship and her sister Mary Queen of Scots' imprisonment were not viewed kindly by the Spanish King. After Elizabeth's marriage refusal and Lepanto, Philip II together with Pope Gregory XIII suggested Mary Stuart as a bride for Don John, as the way of reasserting Catholicism in England. Don John himself was actively involved in attempting to free Mary from prison.[49] English Catholics seemed to be in favour of this match, for if Don John were to marry Mary Queen of Scots he would, through her, be the ruler of a Catholic England.[50]

It also appears that Queen Elizabeth herself sought the attention and affection of Don John. She let it be known in appropriate circles that he might aspire to her hand.[51] Whether Elizabeth's coquetry was personal or political cannot be determined, but, in any event, Don John rebuffed her overtures despite the proddings of the Pope who saw in such a marriage another way to restore England to the Roman fold. In the words of Don John's nineteenth-century biographer, 'Although it is impossible to believe that she had ever seriously thought of marrying him, it is not the less probable that she was much displeased by his refusal even to woo her. She expressed, it is said, great indignation at the slight put upon her by a bastard, and the Spaniards believed that she set on foot plots for his assassination.'⁵²

King James' preface to his youthful account of Lepanto is an elaborate apology attempting to excuse his writing 'in praise of a forraine Papist bastard'.⁵³ Contends James, 'I name not Don-Ioan, neither literally nor any waies by description', and 'my invocation [is] to the true God only, and not to all the He and She Saints, for whose vaine honors, Don-Ioan fought in all his wars'.⁵⁴ One can see by the rigour of James' disclaimers that Don John was not a hero to the English.

Fynes Moryson also describes the negative side of Don John's character from the English point of view when he reports a cruel episode concerning a cave filled with 'ill vapour': 'don John, base sonne of the Emperour Charles the fifth, forced a Gally-slave to goe into this cave, and he falling dead, forced another slave to fetch him out, who likewise fell dead, and that hee killed a third slave with his own hand, because hee refused to fetch out his two dead fellowes'.⁵⁵ Shakespeare's Don John, like Iago resenting the 'daily beauty' in Cassio's life, hates 'the most exquisite Claudio' (I,iii,50), and, with bristling jealousy, labels him 'A proper squire!' (I,iii,52). Hero notes that Don John 'is of a very melancholy disposition' (II,i,5). 'How tartly that gentleman looks!' affirms Beatrice, 'I never can see him but I am heart-burn'd an hour after' (II,i,3–4). The real Don John apparently also had a melancholic temperament.⁵⁶

Though several of Shakespeare's likely sources for *Much Ado About Nothing* are Italian, and an important historical episode involving Italy is in the play's background, the playwright does not call particular attention to his Italian setting except in a most general way. Skirting opportunities to exploit some lurid recent Sicilian family history, as do Beaumont and Fletcher in *Philaster*, or heavy-handed ridicule of Spain, Italy, and Catholicism, as do many a Renaissance English dramatist, Shakespeare is content in *Much Ado About Nothing* to poke at the historical Don John of Austria, and make of Italy a believable comic backdrop.

C THE TEMPEST

The first scene of *The Tempest* is at sea, and the rest of the action takes place on an island – not, that is, in Italy. However, all of the non-fabulous characters in Shakespeare's play are Italian with allegiances to either Milan or Naples. As in *The Two Gentlemen of Verona*, Shakespeare again makes Milan a port city. The usurping Antonio banishes Prospero and Miranda 'to sea' (I,ii,145). Florio's translation of Montaigne's essay 'Des Cannibales' has long been recognized as a source for Gonzalo's reflections on Utopia. The counsellor states that in his

> . . . commonwealth I would by contraries,
> Execute all things; for no kind of traffic
> Would I admit; no name of magistrate;
> Letters should not be known; riches, poverty,
> And use of service, none; contract, succession,
> Bourn, bound of land, tilth, vineyard, none;
> No use of metal, corn, or wine, or oil;
> No occupation, all men idle, all;
> And women too, but innocent and pure;
> No sovereignty –
>
> (II,i,148–57)

Edward Capell, in the eighteenth century, first noticed that Shakespeare's passage about Utopia resembled the following one in Florio's *Montaigne*: 'It is a nation . . . that hath no kinde of traffike, no knowledge of Letters, no intelligence of numbers, no name of magistrate, nor of politike superioritie; no use of service, of riches or of povertie; no contracts, no successions, no partitions, no occupation but idle; no respect of kindred, but common, no apparell but naturall, no manuring of landes, no use of wine, corne, or mettle.'[57] The British Museum copy of Florio's *Montaigne* contains a disputed signature of Shakespeare, but even without any external evidence it seems clear that the playwright read the Frenchman in the Italian's version.

Another possible source for *The Tempest* is Thomas' *The History of Italy*.[58] This work recounts the story of a fifteenth-century Duke of Genoa, Prospero Adorno, with a relevant first name and significant Milanese and Neapolitan connections. Adorno was deposed in 1460, then returned to power seventeen years later by the Duke of Milan. The Genoese Duke subsequently conspired against Milan with the King of Naples, Ferdinando, another interesting name in the context of Shakespeare's play. Tired of constant political intrigue, however, the Genoese people resubmitted themselves to Milan in 1488.

The political motif in *The Tempest* seems the significant link to its Italian background. But unlike most Renaissance English plays set in Italy, revenge, murder, violence, though potential, are held in check in Shakespeare's play. The action takes place in nature, outside, on a magical island, instead of inside an ornate Italian palace. The emphasis in Shakespeare's play is with forgiveness, reconciliation, and love – the ultimate 'magic' that Prospero effects. In their play Romeo and Juliet must die to heal their families' feud; but Ferdinand and Miranda unite both families and countries, presumably to live happily ever after. Removed from Italy, the island setting of *The Tempest* emphasizes essential nature – a paradisal garden, human isolation, the forces of a sea-tempest, passionate love, evil – in the face of the trivial, transitory games so-called 'civilized' people play in the 'City of Man'.

With all the Machiavellian ambition to rule observable in *The Tempest*, one would almost expect a Florentine palace setting for the play or, at least, a Florentine family involvement. But a remote island and families from Milan and Naples serve Shakespeare well enough. Italians were, after all, Italians on the English stage, and Spanish-Italians were more than sufficient.

Prospero has neglected his responsibilities as Duke of Milan, and by shifting them to Antonio has 'Awak'd an evil nature' (I,ii,93) in his brother. Conspiring with the King of Naples to secure his usurped dukedom, Antonio banishes Prospero with his daughter to what seems certain death. On the island during the action of the play, Antonio prods Sebastian into attempting to murder his brother Alonso – 'My strong imagination sees a crown / Dropping upon thy head' (II,i,208–9) – with the motive of ridding Milan of obligation to Naples. Sebastian, after momentary hesitation because of 'conscience' (II,i,275), is persuaded: 'Thy case, dear friend, / Shall be my president: as thou got'st Milan, / I'll come by Naples' (II,i,290–2). Shakespeare has prepared for this Machiavellian maneuvering early in the play, when he shows Antonio and Sebastian nasty characters during the initial storm scene (I,i), and later when they ridicule the good counsellor Gonzalo. These Italians will stop at nothing to rule, even if it means murdering their own brothers. In the end, to be sure, Prospero's magic prevents the assassination (Ariel sings a 'conspiracy' song to wake up Gonzalo and the others [II,i,300–5]), and Prospero 'will tell no tales' (V,i,129) on the traitors. All ends well.

A parallel political plot involves Stephano, who becomes presumed king of the island because of his butt of sack. Caliban thinks him 'a brave god, . . . [who] bears celestial liquor' (II,ii,117). The monster will be a 'true subject, for the liquor is not earthly' (II,ii,125–6). After a while, the fool Trinculo remarks wisely that should the others on the island 'be brain'd like us, the state totters' (III,ii,6–7). (In his works, John Florio often remarked the English propensity for intemperance. Perhaps here, as in *Othello*, Shakespeare was responding by presenting drunken Italians as a rebuttal.[59])

Caliban's plot to kill Prospero mirrors the more serious plan of Antonio and Sebastian to murder Alonso. Prospero rules the island that Caliban thinks rightfully his own: 'This island's mine by Sycorax my mother' (I,ii,331). Prospero's powerful magic is responsible for winning the island from Caliban: 'I say by sorcery he got this isle; / From me he got it' (III,ii,52–3). Prospero never denies that he has usurped, and interestingly accuses Ferdinand of attempting the same thing against him (I,ii,454–7). Caliban wants revenge for the usurpation, and suggests some Italianate-sounding ways to kill Prospero: 'brain him, / . . . or with a log / Batter his skull, or paunch him with a stake, / Or cut his wezand with thy knife' (III,ii,88–91). We are reminded of Lightborn's instruction at Naples.

Besides the pervasive political intrigue in *The Tempest*, very few other Italian details are evident. The comic sequence involving an invisible Ariel speaking for Trinculo (III,ii,42–87) is reminiscent of the so-called 'echo-scene' characteristic of the *Commedia dell'arte*.[60] The device of the illusory banquet, too, is to be found in Italian pastoral drama. When captured in his stolen apparel, Stephano can exclaim to his colleagues, '*Coraggio . . . coraggio!*' (V,i,257–8).

A number of references to the stories and customs of contemporary travel are also to be noted. When Trinculo sees Caliban, he thinks immediately of gain to be derived from exhibiting the monster: 'Were I in England now (as once I was) and had but this fish painted, not a holiday fool there but would give a piece of silver' (II,ii,27–30). Stephano also realizes Caliban's value if he can get him back to Naples, especially since he can speak Italian (II,ii,66–7). The tall tale of the traveller was a commonplace, and the mysterious banquet on the island draws the following comment from Antonio concerning it: 'Travellers ne'er did lie, / Though fools at home condemn 'em' (III,iii,26–7). Gonzalo is convinced that in Naples no one would believe him if he reported the banquet. And yet, Gonzalo remembers, 'When we were boys, / Who would believe that there were mountaineers, / Dew-lapp'd, like bulls, whose throats had hanging at 'em / Wallets of flesh? or that there were such men / Whose heads stood in their breasts?' (III,iii,43–7). Shakespeare was clearly fascinated with traveller stories, and Gonzalo reminds one of Othello's account of his far-flung adventures. The old counsellor adds another note about travel as well: travel gambling or speculation. When he speaks of a 'putter-out of five for one' (III,iii,48–9), Gonzalo is referring to the custom of betting on a dangerous journey. The traveller would deposit a sum of money before his trip, and when and if he returned with proof he had been to the place he had set out for (say, by bringing home a creature from that land) he would be paid perhaps five times his deposit.[61] Of course, many never came back. Fynes Moryson's brother Henry gambled in this manner at three to one.[62]

Most obviously, the island setting of *The Tempest* serves once again as a convenient metaphor for England. James I, like Ferdinand and Miranda, united two kingdoms when he came to England's throne, and James, like Prospero, was a retiring king who shunned public life. Shakespeare, in *Measure for Measure*, had earlier brought this kind of ruler to the stage. England's James, also like Prospero, loved books and the occult. Thus, in one detail or another, as in virtually all of Shakespeare's Italian plays, Italy can be seen as England. The setting for *The Tempest* confirms the connection again.

5
The Undiscovered Country

E. S. Bates cautions wordily but wisely that 'no deduction can be made . . . as to whether Shakespeare ever left England or the reverse, because his capacity for using second-hand knowledge was so unique that it may be said of him as can be said perhaps of no other writer, that it is impossible to make a reasonable guess as to when his knowledge is firsthand and when it is not'.[1] So far there has come to light no documentary evidence whatsoever that Shakespeare visited Italy. For him, it seems, Italy was an 'undiscovered country'. However, this fact has not deterred many commentators from speculating about the possibility of an Italian sojourn.

E. M. Grillo boldly asserts that in a number of plays 'Italy . . . pulsates in every line of our dramatist, while the atmosphere of many scenes is Italian in the truest sense of the word'.[2] His conclusion about Shakespeare as traveller is similarly unflinching: 'on at least one occasion he must have visited Italy'.[3] Other scholars agree. One writes of the playwright's 'eye-witness' verisimilitude and 'intimate description of Italian life', and another of the 'pure Paduan atmosphere' in *The Taming of the Shrew*.[4] But A. Lytton Sells believes the early plays are deficient in detail when compared with, say, *The Merchant of Venice* and those which follow, where 'the Italian local colour is far more precise, more substantial and more convincing'.[5] Einstein also thinks the mature *Othello* shows 'undeniable knowledge of Italy', and that Shakespeare's information about Italian cities is 'remarkable'.[6] Violet Jeffery, too, is sure, for example, that Shakespeare knew Venice firsthand.[7] Contends George Brandes, in sum, Shakespeare's Italy is not 'undiscovered'; it is far more than what might have been gleaned from books or tourists.[8]

The preponderance of critical opinion, however, is on the other side. If most commentators who think Shakespeare travelled are sure he visited the north at least, J. W. Draper is certain he did not: 'Shakespeare never went to northern Italy; and to him the names of famous cities of Lombardy were only names. Most of his [Italian] references are in the early comedies; but, even here, he gives . . . little description beyond the adjective "fair" and a casual allusion to streets [or] walls: . . . the Lombard towns he used merely as glamorous names, and gives them harbors if convenient, or a mountain near at hand if it fitted into the verse.'[9] Indeed, if one compares the journals of Thomas Coryat or Fynes Moryson, or the plays of many Renaissance English playwrights, one is struck with how little detail of Italy there is in Shakespeare's plays.

Supposing for the moment that Shakespeare did in fact travel to Italy, when might he have 'discovered' the country during his busy life? The so-called 'lost years', from about 1585 to about 1592, have been, as could be expected, the most inviting period for speculation. But even here there is debate. Grillo favours the time just after these years, between autumn of 1592 and the summer of 1593, when the plague was rampant and the theatres were closed.[10] This same outbreak of plague still raged in 1594, and Sells notes Shakespeare was associated at this time with the Earl of Southampton – someone who knew the Italian language and had Italian connections.[11] Perhaps this period then? Whatever the time frame, one fact is inescapable to the reader–critic: the playwright never refers to a trip across the Alps, or details a sea journey to Genoa, Venice, or any other Italian port. And it is not too much to assume that given an arduous trip like one to Italy in the late sixteenth or early seventeenth century, Shakespeare would have 'discovered' at least some of the details of it to us in his work.

The Merchant of Venice, usually dated just after the 1593–94 plague period (1596–97), makes specific reference to the Venetian *traghetto*, considered by some a surprisingly accurate detail. Additionally, the 'Lady of Strachy' allusion in *Twelfth Night* is, according to Grillo, an accurate rendering by Shakespeare of an Italian sarcasm referring to a poor but haughty lady – again a remarkably specific reference.[12] Yet 'St. Gregory's Well' in *The Two Gentlemen of Verona*, undoubtedly written earlier, is as noteworthy a detail. And if Padua is not a seaport and Bergamo would not likely breed sailmakers as in *The Taming of the Shrew*, Lombardy *is* very 'fruitful' by all accounts (Coryat, Moryson, etc.) and Padua, in the same play, would be an appropriate place to study. The way from Milan to Mantua might be flat not mountainous as in Shakespeare, not a big mistake, but would Old Gobbo really have a horse in watery Venice? Indeed, Milan as well as Venice is described as a port city in both the early *The Two Gentlemen of Verona* and what could be the last solo play *The*

Tempest. Thus, while there might be an unusually accurate detail of Italian local colour cropping up in this play or that one, from the beginning to the end of Shakespeare's career, the inescapable conclusion is that he was casual about his local colour. But Shakespeare was not the only Renaissance English playwright to get his Italian details wrong at times. John Marston, whose own mother was Italian, makes his Sforzas Venetian not Milanese in *Antonio and Mellida* and *Antonio's Revenge*. George Chapman in *All Fools* puts the Rialto in Florence![13]

What is left out of Shakespeare's Italy, and the playwright's easy reversion to English detail, is perhaps most telling. G. H. McWilliams writes: 'The true explanation of Shakespeare's unconcern for the niceties of geographical accuracy is simply that when he thinks of an urban setting, he is thinking almost exclusively of London.'[14] We have seen indications of this in the plays discussed. It seems clear that Shakespeare did not have everything at hand to flavour his Italian places. Contrast, for example, Marston's lengthy Italian dialogue in *Antonio and Mellida* (IV,i,191–208) with Shakespeare's bookish phrases in *The Taming of the Shrew* (I,ii,24–6, 280; IV,ii,63). There is no Cathedral under construction to grace his Milan (it was finished in the first years of the nineteenth century), no bell tower in Florence, no ruins in Verona, no Arsenal in Venice. Alehouses not wine cellars are the public gathering places. Inn signs include 'Pegasus' and 'Elephant' (only possibly 'Sagittary'). English servants serve Italian masters, and one half-breed, Launcelot Gobbo, dreams not about a plate of pasta but a 'rasher on the coals'. Julio Romano's art was perhaps thought of as sculpture, as one scholar points out, because the word 'sculpsit' was written beneath engraved renderings of his paintings available in England. Another commentator notices that Hoby's *Courtier* translation identifies a sculptor named John Christopher Romano, and suggests Shakespeare may have confused the painter with him.[15]

Ingenious attempts have been made to argue Shakespeare's supposed 'errors' of geography, rather than suggesting an 'undiscovered country', reveal an intimate knowledge of his Italian scenes. The most important of these is Sir Edward Sullivan's essay contending that the playwright knew what he was about when he made apparently inland cities seaports.[16] Sullivan discovered the existence of various Italian waterways connecting several landlocked cities which are ports in Shakespeare's plays. Sullivan's findings, however, have always seemed strained and unconvincing to all but the most willing to believe.

If not first-hand then, where did Shakespeare learn the Italian details he uses? Certainly his sources gave him much of the local colour needed, as can be observed by comparing *Romeo and Juliet* with the Brooke source poem. Bandello, Boccaccio, Cinthio, and others, often by way of translation or adaptation, offered just enough material to create the ambience of Italian places. Einstein is sure that Shakespeare's 'interest in the North can be accounted for in part by his fondness for Bandello and certain of the *novellieri*'.[17] Then, too, many other English playwrights, some with indisputable first-hand knowledge, used Italy as a setting, and Shakespeare must have borrowed here and there from them. English travellers back from Italy, and Thomas' and Coryat's books might have been another fertile source of material, though one wonders why they didn't inspire the playwright to include an Arsenal for military Venice in *Othello* as someone or some book had the Rialto for commercial Venice in *The Merchant of Venice*. The North of Italy was the most popular place to travel on the continent for the English, and perhaps this is why Shakespeare locates the majority of his Italian plays here. Another likely source for detail may have been Shakespeare's fellow actor Robert Armin who was, by all reports, a good Italian scholar. Finally, Shakespeare probably knew some expatriate families, like the Bassanos and Florios, in London.[18] It is highly likely that he was acquainted with John Florio, and, though Florio may never have set foot in Italy, much of his life was dedicated to promoting Italian manners, customs, culture, and language in England.[19] Like Shakespeare, Florio was attached to the Southampton household for a time, and Venice was Italy's foremost city for the translator and dictionary-maker as it was for the playwright. Some critics have found parodies of Florio in a number of Shakespeare's characters; others have found echoes from his works in Shakespeare's dialogue.[20]

One doesn't always ask Shakespeare for perfectly credible plots, and one needn't ask him for perfectly accurate settings. After all, any dramatist's stock-in-trade is to create believable illusions, sometimes from minimal suggestion. Who better of our dramatists might create a 'real' Italy from reading, hearsay, or less? It doesn't really matter if Shakespeare's Italy was 'discovered', if Shakespeare was an Italian traveller. If he were, though, we haven't been able to find his footprints.

Notes

CHAPTER 1: ILLYRIA, ITALIA, ENGLANDIA

1. See Lewis Einstein, *The Italian Renaissance in England* (New York: Columbia University Press, 1902) pp. 366, 367; also F. P. Wilson and G. K. Hunter, *The English Drama 1485–1585* (New York: Oxford University Press, 1969) pp. 114, 137–8.
2. Though John Jeffere's *The Bugbears* (c.1565), which was adapted from A. Grazzini's *La Spiritata* (1561), has some claim.
3. *Gismund of Salerne* may have been acted as early as 1566. The work of Robert Wilmont, Robert Stafford, Henry Noel, G. Al., and Christopher Hatton, it was revised by Wilmont and published in 1591–92 with the title *Tancred and Gismund*. But Arthur Brooke refers to a now lost dramatic precursor to his story in *The Tragical History of Romeus and Juliet* (1562), 'lately set forth on stage'.
4. See The New Arden *Cymbeline*, ed. J. M. Nosworthy (London: Methuen, 1969) pp. xvii–xxv, 191–204.
5. See The New Arden *Twelfth Night*, eds J. M. Lothian and T. W. Craik (London: Methuen, 1975) p. xxxix.
6. Ibid., pp. xxxv–xlvii.
7. Ibid., p. xl.
8. Geoffrey Bullough, *Narrative and Dramatic Sources of Shakespeare*, vol. 2 (London: Routledge & Kegan Paul, 1958) p. 153.
9. *The Italian Renaissance in England*, p. 363.
10. See K. M. Lea, *Italian Popular Comedy*, vol. 2 (Oxford: Oxford University Press, 1934) pp. 431–43.
11. *Shakespeare–Jahrbuch*, 68, pp. 125–7; *Italica*, 23 (1946) pp. 287–93; *The Journal of English and Germanic Philology*, 46 (1947) pp. 75–81; *Revista di Letterature Moderne e Comparate*, N.S. 4 (Jan.–Mar., 1953) pp. 54–8.
12. *Italica*, 23 (1946) pp. 7–17.
13. *Shakespeare Survey 7*, ed. Allardyce Nicoll (Cambridge University Press, 1954) pp. 95–106; reprinted in *The Flaming Heart* (Garden City, N.Y.: Doubleday, 1958) pp. 146–67.
14. *English Studies in Africa*, 4 (1961) pp. 117–27.
15. G. H. McWilliams, *Shakespeare's Italy Revisited* (Leicester University Press, 1974).
16. See The New Arden *Twelfth Night*, pp. xxviii–xxix.
17. *The History of Italy*, ed. George B. Parks (Ithaca, N.Y.: Cornell University Press, 1963). This modern edition is somewhat abridged.
18. See The New Arden *The Tempest*, ed. Frank Kermode (New York: Random House, 1964) pp. lxix–lxx.
19. *The History of Italy*, p. 3.
20. Ed. Edward Arber (London: Constable, 1920) p. 83.
21. Ibid., p. 82.

22. Ibid., p. 78. See also Gabriel Harvey's satiric poem, 'Speculum Tuscanism', on an Italianate Englishman (perhaps Edward de Vere, Earl of Oxford) in *The Works of Gabriel Harvey*, vol. 1, ed. Alexander B. Grosart (New York: AMS Press, 1966 [reprint of 1884 edition]) pp. 84–6.
23. Ibid., p. 78.
24. Thomas Coryat, *Coryat's Crudities*, vol. 1 (Glasgow University Press, 1905).
25. Fynes Moryson, *An Itinerary*, 4 vols (Glasgow University Press, 1907), and *Shakespeare's Europe* (being unpublished chapters of Fynes Moryson's Itinerary [1617]), ed. Charles Hughes (New York: Benjamin Blom, 1967 [reprint of 1903 edn]).
26. *Touring in 1600* (Boston: Houghton Mifflin, 1911) p. 5.
27. *Shakespeare's Europe*, p. iii.
28. J. C. Whitebrook, 'Fynes Moryson, Giordano Bruno and William Shakespeare', *Notes and Queries*, 171 (Oct. 1936) pp. 255–60.
29. *The Works of Thomas Nashe*, vol. 2, ed. Ronald B. McKerrow (London: Sidgwick & Jackson, 1910) p. 297.
30. Ibid., p. 301.
31. See G. K. Hunter, 'English Folly and Italian Vice', in *Jacobean Theatre*, eds John Russell Brown and Bernard Harris (New York: Capricorn Books, 1967) p. 92.
32. *An Itinerary*, vol. 3, pp. 455–6.
33. *English Travellers Abroad 1604–1667* (New York: Octagon Books, 1968 [reprint of 1952 edition]) p. 109. Anthony Munday wrote a celebrated account of his visit to Rome in *The English Romayne Life* (1582), ed. G. B. Harrison (Edinburgh University Press, 1966).
34. 'Shakespeare's Italy', p. 104.

CHAPTER 2: VENICE

1. He is quoting a proverb to be found in John Florio's *First Fruites* (London: Thomas Woodcocke, 1578), p. 34.
2. *The History of Italy*, ed. George B. Parks (Ithaca, N.Y.: Cornell University Press, 1963) p. 63.
3. Ibid., p. 65.
4. *Coryat's Crudities*, vol. 1 (Glasgow University Press, 1905) pp. 303, 306, 302.
5. Ibid., p. 300.
6. John Day, *Humor Out of Breath* (II,i); ed. Arthur Symons, in *Nero and Other Plays* (London: T. Fisher Unwin, 1904) p. 290.
7. *The Scholemaster*, ed. Edward Arber (London: Constable, 1920) p. 84.
8. *The History of Italy*, p. 82.
9. Ibid., p. 82.
10. Ibid., p. 82.
11. Fynes Moryson, *Shakespeare's Europe*, ed. Charles Hughes (New York: Benjamin Blom, 1967 [reprint of 1903 edition]) p. 467.
12. *Coryat's Crudities*, p. 402.
13. *The History of Italy*, p. 82.

Notes to pp. 13–20

14. *Coryat's Crudities*, pp. 387–8.
15. *Shakespeare's Europe*, p. 412.
16. Ibid., pp. 129–30.
17. *The History of Italy*, pp. 82–3.
18. *Shakespeare's Europe*, pp. 412–13.
19. *Coryat's Crudities*, p. 400.
20. Ibid., p. 399.
21. Ibid., p. 280.
22. Ibid., p. 386.
23. *Shakespeare's Europe*, p. 417.
24. *An Itinerary*, vol. 3 (Glasgow University Press, 1907) p. 413.
25. See John Walter Stoye, *English Travellers Abroad 1604–1667* (New York: Octagon Books, 1968 [reprint of 1952 edition]) pp. 113–14.
26. See E. S. Bates, *Touring in 1600* (Boston: Houghton-Mifflin, 1911) pp. 27–8.
27. *Coryat's Crudities*, p. 380.
28. *The History of Italy*, p. 69.
29. *Shakespeare's Europe*, p. 153.
30. See John W. Draper, 'Shakespeare and the Doge of Venice', *The Journal of English and Germanic Philology*, 46 (1947) p. 78.
31. *Coryat's Crudities*, p. 326.
32. *The Unfortunate Traveller*, in *The Works of Thomas Nashe*, vol. 2, ed. Ronald B. McKerrow (London: Sidgwick & Jackson, 1910) p. 243.
33. *John Webster: Three Plays*, ed. D. C. Gunby (New York: Penguin Books, 1972) p. 416.
34. *Touring in 1600*, p. 56.
35. *John Florio* (Cambridge University Press, 1934) p. 281.
36. *Shakespeare's Europe*, pp. 424–5.
37. *Second Frutes* (London: Thomas Woodcocke, 1591) p. 141.
38. 'Shakespeare's Italy', in *Shakespeare Survey 7*, ed. Allardyce Nicoll (Cambridge University Press, 1954) p. 106; 'Englishmen in Padua, from Chaucer to Shelley', *Durham University Journal*, N.S. 9 (Dec. 1947) p. 4.
39. *An Itinerary*, vol. 1 (Glasgow University Press, 1907) p. 374.
40. Violet M. Jeffery notes that 'Belmont calls to mind the palace of Caterina Cornaro at Asolo, or one of the country residences which lined the banks of the river Brenta.' 'Shakespeare's Venice', *Modern Language Review*, 27 (Jan. 1932) p. 28. Thomas Coryat also remarks the Brenta river and villas. *Coryat's Crudities*, pp. 269, 300.
41. *Coryat's Crudities*, p. 282.
42. *Shakespeare's Europe*, p. 149.
43. Ibid., p. 467.
44. *Coryat's Crudities*, p. 364.
45. Though since both Moryson and Coryat mention this ferryboat, it must have been well-known. See *An Itinerary*, vol. 1, p. 164, and *Coryat's Crudities*, p. 311.
46. *The History of Italy*, p. 66; *Shakespeare's Europe*, p. 459.
47. *Coryat's Crudities*, p. 312.
48. Ibid., p. 304.

49. Ibid., p. 309.
50. *An Itinerary*, vol. 1, p. 191. See also vol. 3, p. 487.
51. *Narrative and Dramatic Sources of Shakespeare*, vol. 1, ed. Geoffrey Bullough (London: Routledge & Kegan Paul, 1957) p. 473.
52. 'Shakespeare's Italy', p. 104.
53. *The History of Italy*, p. 108.
54. *Shakespeare's Europe*, p. 136.
55. Ibid., p. 136.
56. Ibid., p. 141.
57. Ibid., p. 135.
58. Ibid., p. 135.
59. Quoted in Lewis Einstein, *The Italian Renaissance in England* (New York: Columbia University Press, 1902) p. 269.
60. See Benjamin N. Nelson, 'The Usurer and the Merchant Prince: Italian Businessmen and the Ecclesiastical Law of Restitution, 1100–1550', *Journal of Economic History*, 7 (1947) p. 117. Moryson notes that 'not only the Gentlemen, but even the Prince of Italy openly professe to be merchants'. *An Itinerary*, vol. 4, p. 88.
61. *Coryat's Crudities*, p. 314.
62. Ibid., pp. 318, 314.
63. *The History of Italy*, p. 83.
64. *The Scholemaster*, p. 86.
65. *An Itinerary*, vol. 1, p. 192. See also *Shakespeare's Europe*, p. 488.
66. *Coryat's Crudities*, p. 370.
67. *Shakespeare's Europe*, p. 489. See also *Coryat's Crudities*, p. 370.
68. Ibid., p. 487.
69. Ibid., p. 488.
70. Ibid., pp. 487, 488.
71. Ibid., p. 160.
72. *The History of Italy*, p. 69.
73. Coryat describes Jewish women: 'some were as beautiful as ever I saw'. *Coryat's Crudities*, p. 372.
74. *Shakespeare's Europe*, p. 157.
75. Ibid., p. 429.
76. Ibid., p. 424.
77. *The History of Italy*, p. 77.
78. Quoted from The New Arden *The Merchant of Venice*, ed. John Russell Brown (New York: Random House, 1964) p. 149.
79. See 'Shakespeare and the Doge of Venice', p. 78. Yet, surprisingly, Shakespeare does know that the Doge had a double vote in the Venetian Council, p. 80. See also J. W. Draper, 'Some Details of Italian Local Colour in "Othello"', *Shakespeare–Jahrbuch*, 68, p. 125.
80. The confiscation of goods, in fact, was part of the conversion process. See *Coryat's Crudities*, pp. 373–4.
81. Quoted from The New Arden *The Merchant of Venice*, p. 170.
82. *The Works of Thomas Nashe*, vol. 2, p. 305.
83. *Coryat's Crudities*, p. 372.
84. *Shakespeare's Europe*, p. 33.
85. Robert Marx, *The Battle of Lepanto, 1571* (Cleveland: World, 1966) p. 67.

Notes to pp. 29–40   95

86. Ibid., p. 68.
87. John Francis Guilmartin, Jr, *Gunpowder and Galleys* (Cambridge University Press, 1974) p. 250.
88. See Violet M. Jeffery, 'Shakespeare's Venice', pp. 24–35; and J. W. Draper, 'Some Details of Italian Local Colour in "Othello"', pp. 125–7.
89. *The History of Italy*, p. 66.
90. See *Shakespeare's Europe*, pp. 143–5, and *Coryat's Crudities*, p. 358.
91. *The History of Italy*, p. 78.
92. Quoted from *Narrative and Dramatic Sources of Shakespeare*, vol. 7 (London: Routledge & Kegan Paul, 1973) p. 245.
93. *Shakespeare's Europe*, p. 404.
94. *The Unfortunate Traveller*, in *The Works of Thomas Nashe*, vol. 2, p. 326.
95. *The History of Italy*, p. 82.
96. *Shakespeare's Europe*, pp. 150–1.
97. See J. W. Draper, 'Shakespeare and the Doge of Venice', pp. 78–81.
98. See note in The New Arden *Othello*, ed. M. R. Ridley (New York: Random House, 1967) p. 48.
99. See J. W. Draper, 'Shakespeare and Florence and the Florentines', *Italica*, 23 (1946) pp. 291–2.
100. See *John Florio*, p. 117. Fynes Moryson writes, 'The Italians hold it a great shame to be drunken'. *An Itinerary*, vol. 4 (Glasgow University Press, 1907) p. 102. See also vol. 3, p. 374.
101. *Shakespeare's Europe*, p. 415. See also *An Itinerary*, vol. 1, p. 351.
102. *The History of Italy*, p. 96.
103. See Theodore C. Hoepfner, 'Iago's Nationality', *Notes and Queries*, N.S. vol. 2 (Jan. 1955) pp. 14–15.
104. *Narrative and Dramatic Sources of Shakespeare*, vol. 7, pp. 246–7.
105. Note the interesting similarity of language in Fynes Moryson: 'In general it is said of the Italian women: . . . They are Magpyes at the doore, Saints in the church, Goates in the garden, Divels in the house, Angels in the streets, and Syrens at the window'. *An Itinerary*, vol. 3, p. 459.
106. *English Travellers Abroad 1604–1667*, p. 109.
107. *Shakespeare's Europe*, p. 409.
108. *The Unfortunate Traveller*, in *The Works of Thomas Nashe*, vol. 2, p. 301.
109. For clinical discussions of Iago, see Martin Wangh, 'Othello: the Tragedy of Iago', *Psychoanalytic Quarterly*, 19 (1950) pp. 202–12; Gordon Ross Smith, 'Iago the Paranoic', *American Imago*, 16 (1959) pp. 155–67; and, especially, Stanley Edgar Hyman, *Iago: Some Approaches to the Illusion of His Motivation* (New York: Atheneum, 1970) pp. 101–21.

CHAPTER 3: THE TERRA FIRMA

1. *The Scholemaster*, ed. Edward Arber (London: Constable, 1920) p. 61.
2. Ibid., p. 72.
3. Ibid., p. 74.

Notes to pp. 40–7

4. Ibid., p. 79.
5. Ibid., p. 79.
6. Ibid., p. 66.
7. Ibid., p. 85.
8. Ibid., p. 78.
9. Quoted in Clare Howard, *English Travellers of the Renaissance* (London: John Lane, 1914) p. 73.
10. Ibid., p. 98.
11. *An Itinerary*, vol. 3 (Glasgow University Press, 1907) p. 349.
12. Ibid., p. 359.
13. Fynes Moryson, *Shakespeare's Europe*, ed. Charles Hughes (New York: Benjamin Blom, 1967 [reprint of 1903 edition]) p. 430. See also *An Itinerary*, vol. 1 (Glasgow University Press, 1907) pp. 156, 333. Thomas Coryat missed the University when in Padua. See *Coryat's Crudities*, vol. 1 (Glasgow University Press, 1905) p. 296.
14. *Shakespeare's Europe*, p. 430.
15. Ibid., p. 129. See also *An Itinerary*, vol. 1, p. 380.
16. *Shakespeare's Europe*, p. 163.
17. *The History of Italy*, ed. George B. Parks (Ithaca, N.Y.: Cornell University Press, 1963) p. 11.
18. Quoted in John Walter Stoye, *English Travellers Abroad 1604–1667* (New York: Octagon Books, 1968 [reprint of 1952 edition]) p. 142.
19. *Coryat's Crudities*, p. 283; see also pp. 237–9, 245, 384.
20. Ibid., p. 274.
21. *Zelauto: The Fountaine of Fame*, ed. Jack Stillinger (Carbondale, Ill.: Southern Illinois University Press, 1963) p. 113. In this third part of Munday's work, Strabino is sent to Verona 'to be trayned up in such vertuous educations; as was meete for one of his tender time'.
22. Quoted from Geoffrey Bullough, *Narrative and Dramatic Sources of Shakespeare*, vol. 1 (London: Routledge & Kegan Paul, 1957) p. 286.
23. *An Itinerary*, vol. 1, p. 377.
24. Ibid., p. 377.
25. See J. W. Draper, 'Shakespeare and the Lombard Cities', *Revista di Letterature Moderne e Comparate*, N.S. 4 (Jan.–Mar. 1953) pp. 55–6.
26. *Coryat's Crudities*, pp. 262, 264. See also *An Itinerary*, vol. 1, pp. 378–9.
27. *Touring in 1600* (Boston: Houghton Mifflin, 1911) p. 102.
28. *The History of Italy*, pp. 112–13.
29. *The Diary of John Evelyn*, ed. E. S. de Beer (London: Oxford University Press, 1959) p. 252.
30. *The History of Italy*, p. 114.
31. See *Narrative and Dramatic Sources of Shakespeare*, vol. 1, pp. 111, 73; and, especially, The New Arden *The Taming of the Shrew*, ed. Brian Morris (London: Methuen, 1981) pp. 12–50, 65–88.
32. See Lewis Einstein, *The Italian Renaissance in England* (New York: Columbia University Press, 1902) p. 190.
33. *Shakespeare's Europe*, p. 154.
34. See the section on the education theme in The New Arden *The Taming of the Shrew*, pp. 129–33.

35. See Morris' analysis of Petruchio's teaching methods in The New Arden *The Taming of the Shrew*, pp. 131–2.
36. *The Civile Conversation of M. Steeven Guazzo*, vol. 2, ed. Edward Sullivan (London: Constable, 1925) p. 80.
37. *Shakespeare's Europe*, pp. 251–2.
38. See Frances A. Yates, *John Florio* (Cambridge University Press, 1934) pp. 147–73.
39. Fynes Moryson, for example, goes to Florence for money. *An Itinerary*, vol. 1, pp. 307, 316; see also J. W. Draper, 'Shakespeare and Florence and the Florentines', *Italica*, 23 (1946) p. 288.
40. *Shakespeare's Europe*, p. 434.
41. 'Shakespeare and the Lombard Cities', p. 57.
42. 'Shakespeare and Italy' in *The Secondary Heroes of Shakespeare and Other Essays* (London: Kingswood Press, 1950) p. 89.
43. 'Shakespeare's Italy' in *Shakespeare Survey 7*, ed. Allardyce Nicoll Cambridge University Press, 1954) p. 100.
44. Ibid., p. 100.
45. 'Shakespeare and Italy' in *English Studies in Africa*, 4 (1961) p. 124.
46. *Shakespeare's Europe*, p. 458.
47. Ibid., p. 460. See also Moryson, *An Itinerary*, vol. 1, p. 158.
48. *Coryat's Crudities*, p. 393.
49. *Shakespeare's Europe*, p. 456.
50. *The Scholemaster*, p. 72. See also Moryson, *An Itinerary*, vol. 3, pp. 401–3, 407.
51. *Coryat's Crudities*, p. 413.
52. *Shakespeare's Europe*, p. 463. See also *Coryat's Crudities*, pp. 413–14.
53. *Shakespeare's Europe*, p. 407. Moryson also recounts a love story against the background of factious families which roughly parallels *Romeo and Juliet*. See *An Itinerary*, vol. 1, pp. 318–19.
54. See The New Arden *Romeo and Juliet*, ed. Brian Gibbons (London: Methuen, 1980) pp. 32–42.
55. *The Posies*, ed. John W. Cunliffe (Cambridge University Press, 1907) p. 83.
56. See M. C. Bradbrook, *Shakespeare: the Poet in His World* (New York: Columbia University Press, 1978) pp. 100–1, 244n.
57. *Shakespeare's Europe*, pp. 402–3.
58. Silver's book has been reprinted, with an introduction by J. Dover Wilson (London: Oxford University Press, 1933); Saviolo's was published in London and printed by John Wolfe.
59. *Paradoxes of Defence*, 'Dedicatorie'.
60. John Florio, *First Fruites* (London: Thomas Woodcocke, 1578) pp. 17–18.
61. See The New Arden *The Two Gentlemen of Verona*, ed. Clifford Leech (London: Methuen, 1969) pp. xliii–xliv.
62. Ibid., p. xxxviii.
63. Ibid., p. xxxix.
64. *Euphues*, in *The Complete Works of John Lyly*, vol. 1, ed. R. Warwick Bond (Oxford University Press, 1902) p. 185.

65. Ibid., p. 197.
66. Ibid., p. 209.
67. See The New Arden *The Two Gentlemen of Verona*, pp. xiii–xxi.
68. *The History of Italy*, pp. 115–18.
69. Ibid., p. 112.
70. See The New Arden *The Two Gentlemen of Verona*, p. 89n.
71. *Shakespearian Comedy* (New York: Macmillan, 1938) p. 83.
72. *Shakespeare's Europe*, p. 410.
73. Ibid., p. 410.

CHAPTER 4: BEYOND THE SIGNORY

1. J. W. Stoye, *English Travellers Abroad 1604–1667* (New York: Octagon Books, 1968 [reprint of 1952 edition]) p. 119.
2. E. S. Bates, *Touring in 1600* (Boston: Houghton Mifflin, 1911) p. 103.
3. *The History of Italy*, ed. George B. Parks (Ithaca, N.Y.: Cornell University Press, 1963) p. 98.
4. Ibid., pp. 93–4. Fynes Moryson describes Florence as 'a most sweet City, and abounding with wealth, the Citizens are much commended for their courtesie, modesty, gravity, purity of language, and many virtues'. *An Itinerary*, vol. 1 (Glasgow University Press, 1907) p. 316.
5. *The History of Italy*, p. 93.
6. Lewis Einstein, *The Italian Renaissance in England* (New York: Columbia University Press, 1902) p. 95.
7. *Shakespeare's Europe*, ed. Charles Hughes (New York: Benjamin Blom, 1967 [reprint of 1903 edition]) p. 145.
8. 'Shakespeare's Italy' in *Shakespeare Survey 7* (Cambridge University Press, 1954) p. 104.
9. *Touring in 1600*, p. 113.
10. *English Travellers Abroad*, p. 124.
11. In *The Two Gentlemen of Verona*, however, it is '*Don* Antonio' (II,iv,54).
12. *The History of Italy*, p. 87.
13. *The Scholemaster*, ed. Edward Arber (London: Constable, 1920) p. 85; *The Complete Works of John Lyly*, vol. 1, ed. R. Warwick Bond (Oxford University Press, 1902) p. 189.
14. *The Complete Works of John Lyly*, vol. 1, pp. 241, 240.
15. *Shakespeare's Europe*, pp. 418, 436.
16. *The History of Italy*, p. 90.
17. Ibid., p. 89.
18. Ibid., pp. 90, 89.
19. *The Unfortunate Traveller*, in *The Works of Thomas Nashe*, vol. 2, ed. Ronald B. McKerrow (London: Sidgwick & Jackson, 1910) p. 298.
20. *The History of Italy*, p. 90.
21. *Shakespeare's Europe*, p. 131.
22. Ibid., p. 137.
23. The New Arden *The Tempest* (New York: Random House, 1964) p. 1.
24. *The History of Italy*, p. 97.
25. *Shakespeare's Europe*, p. 99.

Notes to pp. 71–82

26. See *The History of Italy*, p. 96.
27. The modern edition is edited by Allan Gilbert, in *Machiavelli: The Chief Works and Others*, vol. 2 (Durham, N.C.: Duke University Press, 1965) pp. 705, 716–17.
28. See The New Arden *All's Well That Ends Well*, ed. G. K. Hunter (London: Methuen, 1967) p. xxix.
29. Ibid., p. xxv.
30. See E. G. Withycombe, *The Oxford Dictionary of English Christian Names* (Oxford University Press, 1973) p. 141.
31. See F. G. Holweck, *A Biographical Dictionary of the Saints* (Detroit: Gale Research, 1969 [reprint of 1924 edition]) p. 467.
32. *The History of Italy*, p. 13.
33. See the discussion of sources in The New Arden *Much Ado About Nothing*, ed. A. R. Humphreys (London: Methuen, 1981) pp. 5–25. See also Charles T. Prouty, *The Sources of Much Ado About Nothing* (New Haven, Conn.: Yale University Press, 1950).
34. The New Arden *Much Ado About Nothing*, p. 50.
35. Ibid., p. 50.
36. 'Shakespeare and Florence and the Florentines', *Italica*, 23 (1946) p. 289.
37. This might answer A. R. Humphreys' question, in his 'Introduction' to The New Arden *Much Ado About Nothing*, as to 'why Benedick hails from Padua', p. 65.
38. Robert M. Adams (New York: Norton, 1977) p. xvi.
39. See Mary Augusta Scott, 'The Book of the Courtier: a Possible Source of Benedick and Beatrice', *PMLA*, 16 (1901) pp. 475–502; also, A. R. Humphreys, The New Arden *Much Ado About Nothing*, pp. 16–19. Fynes Moryson notes: 'The Italian women are said to bee sharpe witted . . .' *An Itinerary*, vol. 3 (Glasgow University Press, 1908) p. 452.
40. The Blackfriars Shakespeare *Much Ado About Nothing* (Dubuque, Iowa: William C. Brown, 1969) p. xiv.
41. See *The Italian Renaissance in England*, p. 108.
42. Ibid., p. 80.
43. *The History of Italy*, p. 16.
44. See John Francis Guilmartin, Jr, *Gunpowder and Galleys* (Cambridge University Press, 1974) pp. 221–52, *passim*. Also, Robert Marx, *The Battle of Lepanto, 1571* (Cleveland: World, 1966).
45. *Gunpowder and Galleys*, p. 234.
46. The one for the Montague weddings referred to in Chapter 3. See *The Posies*, ed. John C. Cunliffe (Cambridge University Press, 1907) pp. 75–86.
47. Abraham Holland, *Naumachia. or, A Poeticall Description* . . . (London, 1622). STC 13580.
48. 'The Lepanto of James the sixt, King of Scotland' in *His Majesties Poetical Exercises at Vacant Houres* (Edinburgh).
49. William Stirling-Maxwell, *Don John of Austria*, vol. 2 (London: Longmans Green, 1833) p. 22.
50. Ibid., p. 22.
51. Ibid., p. 287.
52. Ibid., p. 287.

53. 'The Lepanto of James the sixt, King of Scotland'.
54. Ibid.
55. *An Itinerary*, vol. 1, p. 243.
56. *Don John of Austria*, vol. 2, p. 24.
57. Quoted in Frances A. Yates, *John Florio* (Cambridge University Press, 1934) pp. 242–3.
58. See the New Arden *The Tempest*, pp. lxix–lxv.
59. See *John Florio*, p. 116.
60. See K. M. Lea, *Italian Popular Comedy*, vol. 2 (Oxford University Press, 1934) pp. 443–53; also, The New Arden *The Tempest*, pp. lxvii–lxix.
61. In Ben Jonson's *Every Man Out of His Humour*, the vain knight Puntarvolo comments on a travel plan: 'I am determined to put forth some five thousand pound, to be paid me five for one, upon the return of myself, my wife, and my dog from the Turk's court in Constantinople. If all or either of us miscarry in the journey, 'tis gone: if we be successful, why, there will be five and twenty thousand pound to entertain time withal' (II,i).
62. *Shakespeare's Europe*, pp. xiv–xv.

CHAPTER 5: THE UNDISCOVERED COUNTRY

1. *Touring in 1600* (Boston: Houghton Mifflin, 1911) p. 87.
2. *Shakespeare and Italy* (Glasgow University Press, 1949) p. 132.
3. Ibid., p. 132.
4. Quoted in Mario Praz, 'Shakespeare's Italy' in *Shakespeare Survey 7* (Cambridge University Press, 1954) p. 96.
5. 'Englishmen in Padua, from Chaucer to Shelley', *The Durham University Journal*, 40 (Dec. 1947) p. 5.
6. Lewis Einstein, *The Italian Renaissance in England* (New York: Columbia University Press, 1902) p. 396.
7. 'Shakespeare's Venice', *Modern Language Review*, 27 (Jan. 1932) pp. 24–35.
8. See Praz, 'Shakespeare's Italy', p. 96.
9. 'Shakespeare and the Lombard Cities', *Revista di Letterature Moderne e Comparate*, N.S. 4 (Jan.–Mar. 1953) p. 58.
10. *Shakespeare and Italy*, p. 133.
11. 'Englishmen in Padua, from Chaucer to Shelley', p. 4.
12. *Shakespeare and Italy*, p. 32.
13. George Chapman, *All Fools* (V,ii,16); ed. Frank Manley (Lincoln, Nebr.: University of Nebraska Press, 1968).
14. *Shakespeare's Italy Revisited* (Leicester University Press, 1974) p. 17.
15. See A. C. Partridge, 'Shakespeare and Italy', *English Studies in Africa*, 4 (1961) p. 119; also D. E. Baughan, 'Shakespeare's Confusion of the two Romanos', *Journal of English and Germanic Philology*, 36 (Jan. 1937) pp. 35–9, and Mary Augusta Scott, 'The Book of the Courtier: a Possible Source of Benedick and Beatrice', *PMLA*, 16 (1901) pp. 478, 481.
16. *The Nineteenth Century*, 64 (Aug. 1908).
17. *The Italian Renaissance in England*, p. 370.

18. See Barbara D. G. Steer, 'Shakespeare and Italy', *Notes and Queries*, 198 (Jan. 1953) p. 23; and, A. L. Rowse, *The Poems of Shakespeare's Dark Lady* (London: Jonathan Cape, 1978) pp. 1–37.
19. See Frances A. Yates, *John Florio* (Cambridge University Press, 1934) *passim*.
20. Ibid., pp. 334–6.

Index

Aaron, *TA*, 8
Adam, *TS*, 52
Adams, Robert M., 99n38
Adige river (Verona), 11
Adorni, 55
Adorno, Prospero (Duke of Genoa), 5, 83
Aguecheek, Sir Andrew, *TN*, 11, 77
alehouses (English detail), 11, 31, 62, 78, 89
Al., G., 91n3
All Fools, 2, 65, 89
All's Well That Ends Well, 2, 7, 9, 66, 69, 70–6
Alonso, *T*, 10, 67, 69, 70, 84, 85
Alphonso, Don, *TGV*, 45
Alps, 88
Aminta, 3
Amphitheatre and Roman ruins (Verona), 11
Andrugio, *Antonio and Mellida* and *Antonio's Revenge*, 15
Angelo, *MM*, 3
Anglo-Spanish Treaty (1604), 67
Anthony, *RJ*, 57
Antonio, *AWEW*, 72
Antonio, *Antonio and Mellida* and *Antonio's Revenge*, 15
Antonio, *MAAN*, 79
Antonio, *MV*, 10, 15, 19–27 *passim*
Antonio, *T*, 11, 70, 83, 84, 85
Antonio, Don, *TGV*, 45, 61, 62
Antonio and Mellida, 15, 89
Antonio's Revenge, 15, 89
Apothecary, *RJ*, 44
Aquilano, Serafino, 54
Aragon, House of, 66
Arber, Edward, 91ns20–1, 92ns22–3,7, 95ns1–3, 96ns4–8, 98n13
Arezzo, 65
Ariel, *T*, 84, 85
Ariosto, 2, 9, 76

Aristotle, 46
Armado, Don Adriano de, *LLL*, 3
Armin, Robert, 90
Arno river (Florence), 11, 70
Arqua, 18
Arragon, Cardinal of, *The White Devil*, 66
Arragon, Prince of, *MV*, 28, 66
Arsenal (Venice), 16, 31, 89, 90
The Art of War, 9, 65, 71
Ascham, Roger, 6, 7, 12, 21, 28, 40–2, 47, 55, 67
As You Like It, 3, 5, 51
Athens, 46, 61
Athesis river (Verona), 44

badges (for Jews), 21
Bacci, 66
Baglione, Astor, 30
Balthazar, *MAAN*, 79
Bandello, Matteo, 3, 76–7, 90
Baptista, *H*, 3
Barabas, *The Jew of Malta*, 22–3, 28, 34
Bassanio, *MV*, 10, 18, 24, 25
Bassano (family), 90
Bassano (Jacopo da Ponte), 18
Bassano del Grappa, 18
Bastard, *KJ*, 8
Bates, E. S., 6, 45, 87, 93n26, 98n2
Battle of Campaldino (1289), 65
The Battle of Lepanto, 1571, 94n85, 95n86, 99n44
Battle of Lepanto (1571), 30, 80–2
Baughan, D. E., 100n15
Bay of Naples, 67
Beatrice, *MAAN*, 7, 8, 69, 78, 79, 82
Beaumont and Fletcher, 2, 82
Bellario, *MV*, 20
Bell Tower (Florence), 70, 89
Belleforest, François, 76
Belmont, 18, 23, 24, 25, 28, 29, 30

Index

Benedick, *MAAN*, 7, 10, 69, 77, 78, 79
Bentivolii family, 52
Benvolio, *RJ*, 57, 60
Bergamo, 52, 88
Bertram, *AWEW*, 10, 42, 66, 69, 72–6
Beverley, Peter, 76
Bianca (Moryson), 46
Bianca, *O*, 8, 10, 34, 36, 38
Bianca, *TS*, 10, 47–52 *passim*
Bianchi, 46, 55
A Biographical Dictionary of the Saints, 99n31
The Blackfriars Shakespeare *Much Ado About Nothing*, 99n40
Boccaccio, 2, 71, 90
Bocchi, 66
Bologna, 5, 20
Bolognese, 52
Bolognian sausages (*Volpone*), 16
Bond, R. Warwick, 97n64, 98ns65–6,13
'The Book of the Courtier: a Possible Source of Benedick and Beatrice', 99n39, 100n15
Borachio, *MAAN*, 78, 79
Borgia (family), 8
Brabantio, *O*, 10, 30, 32–3
Bracciano, Duke of (Don Virginio Orsino), 5
Bradbrook, M. C., 56, 97n56
Bragadino, Marc Antonio, 30
Brandes, George, 87
Braun, Georg, 62
Brenta river and canal, 18
British Museum copy of Florio's *Montaigne*, 83
Brooke, Arthur, 43–4, 60, 63, 90, 91n3
Brown, John Russell, 92n31
Brown, Sir Anthony, 5
The Bugbears, 91n2
Bullingbroke, *RII*, 8
Bullough, Geoffrey, 91n8, 94n51, 96n22
Burton Heath, 53

Caius, John, 42

Calamech, Andrea, 80
Caliban, *T*, 10, 69–70, 85
Cambio (Lucentio) *TS*, 47, 48
Cambridge, University of, 6
Cancellieri, 55
Candia (Crete), 29
Capell, Edward, 83
Capilet, Diana, *AWEW*, 71, 75, 76
Capilet, Old Widow, *AWEW*, 71
Captain, *TN*, 1
Capulet (family), *RJ*, 54, 59, 78
Capulet, Old, *RJ*, 10
Capulet and Montague feud, 56
Carafa, 66
Cassio, *O*, 9, 31–8 *passim*, 77, 82
Castiglione, Baldassare, 9, 23, 40, 44, 78–9
Cathedral of Florence, 70
Cathedral of Milan (Duomo), 45, 62, 89
Catling, Simon, *RJ*, 57
Cecil, William (Lord Burghley), 41
Celia, *Volpone*, 16, 17
Cervantes, 80
chapineys, 13
Chapman, George, 2, 65, 89
Charlecote Manor, 11
Charles V, Emperor, 82
Charles VIII, 67
Charlton, H. B., 62
Chlorus, Constantine, 74
Cinthio, Giraldi, 3, 31, 35, 36, 90
'Circe's Court' (Italy), 67
circumcision, 27–8
Civile Conversation of M. Steeven Guazzo, 48, 97n36
Civitates Orbis Terrarum, 62
Claudio, *MAAN*, 9, 10, 69, 77–9 *passim*, 82
Claudio, *MM*, 3
Claudio and Hero plot, 76
Clown, *AWEW*, 71, 75
Clown, *O*, 36
Coelus (Earl of Colchester), 74
The Comedy of Errors, 2
Commedia dell'arte, 3, 51, 62, 77, 85
The Complete Works of John Lyly, 97n64, 98n65, ns66,13
Conrade, *MAAN*, 79

Constantine, Emperor, 74
Constantinople, 29
conversion theme, *MV*, 22, 25–9
Corombona, Vittoria, *The White Devil*, 15
Corte, 56
Il Cortegiano, 40, 78, see The Courtier
Coryat, Thomas, 6, 12–15 *passim*, 18–21 *passim*, 28, 31, 43, 44, 54, 55, 88, 90, 92–7 *passim*
Coryat's Crudities, 6, 92–7 *passim*
Countess, *AWEW*, 10, 72, 74, 75
courtesans, 6, 8, 12–17 *passim*, 22, 23, 31, 33, 36, 38, 63, 76
The Courtier, 89, see *Il Cortegiano*
Crab, *TGV*, 63
Cunliffe, John W., 97n55, 99n46
Cupid, 77
Curtis, *TS*, 47, 52
Cymbeline, 2
Cyprus, 29–30, 32, 37

Dante, 42, 56, 65
Danvers, Charles, 56–7
Danvers, Henry, 56–7
Day, John, 12
de Beer, E. S., 96n29
Decameron, 2, 71
'Dedicatorie' to *Paradoxes of Defence*, 97n59
Dekker, Thomas, 2
'Des Cannibales' (Montaigne), 83
Desdemona, *O*, 10, 17, 30, 32–9 *passim*, 58
de Vere, Edward (Earl of Oxford), 92n22
The Diary of John Evelyn, 96n29
Discorso, 66
'Dobbin', *MV*, 19
Dogberry, *MAAN*, 66, 78
Don John of Austria, 99ns49–52, 100n56
Draper, John W., 3, 52, 77, 87, 93n30, 94n79, 95n88, 97, 99, 96n25, 97n39
Drummond, William (of Hawthornden), 15
Duchess of Malfi, *Duchess of Malfi*, 79

Duke, *Antonio's Revenge*, 15
Duke, *MV*, 14, 26–7
Duke, *O*, 15, 31, 33
Duke, *TGV*, 60–4 *passim*
Duke of Florence, *AWEW*, 66
Duke of Florence, *The White Devil*, 65
Durham University Journal, 93n38, 100n5

eavesdropping motif in *MAAN*, 78
'echo-scene', 85
Edgar, *KL*, 60
Edmund, *KL*, 8
Edward II, 68, 79
Edward VI, King, 42, 66
Edwardes, Richard, 57, 60
Eglamour, Sir, *TGV*, 64
Einstein, Lewis, 87, 90, 91n1, 94n59, 96n32, 98n6, 100n6
'The Elephant' (Inn), 11, 89
Eliot, John, 50
Elizabeth I, Queen, 5, 23, 42, 46, 80–2 *passim*
Emilia, *O*, 34, 36
Emilia, Lady, *Il Cortegiano*, 78
England, 14–15, 23, 40–1, 79, 81, 85, 86
English
  Catholics, 81
  details, 11, 19, 31, 52, 53, 57, 62, 77–8, 79, 89
  intemperance, 33, 85
  interest in Italy, 23
  law, 14–15, 26–7
  names, 11, 19, 52, 57, 58, 62, 78
  Parliament, 14–15
  riding customs, 68–9
  songs, 31, 52, 57, 78
  stereotype of Italians, 19, 31
  styles, 52, 79
  travel to Italy, 5–7, 40–2
  values, 41
The English Drama, 1485–1585, 91n1
'English Folly and Italian Vice', 92n31
The English Romayne Life, 92n33
English Studies in Africa, 91n14, 97n45, 100n15

Index

English Travellers Abroad 1604–1667, 92n33, 93n25, 95n106, 96n18, 98ns1,10
English Travellers of the Renaissance, 96n9
'Englishmen in Padua, from Chaucer to Shelley', 93n38, 100ns5,11
'Englishmen Italianated', 11, 40–1
Epitia, *Hecatommithi*, 3
Escalus, *AWEW*, 72
Escalus, Prince (Escala), *RJ*, 44
Essex, Earl of, 57
Eudaf, 74
Euganean Hills, 18
Euphues, 7, 48, 61, 67, 97n64
Euphues, 61, 67
Evelyn, John, 45
Every Man Out of His Humour, 100n61
The Excellent Comedy of Two Most Faithful Friends, Damon and Pithias, 60

Famagusta, 29
Faust situation, 24, 73
female and generative references in Iago's diction, 37–8
Ferdinand, *T*, 10, 41, 70, 84, 85, 86
Ferdinando (King of Naples), 83
Ferrabosco, Alfonso, 5
Ferrara, 46
Finddu, Owen, 74
First Fruites, 50, 57, 92n1
The Flaming Heart, 91n13
Florence, 2, 5, 9, 11, 13, 33–5, 45, 51, 65–6, 69, 70–1, 75, 89
Florence, Duke of, 66, 71
Florence, Duke of, *AWEW*, 66
Florentine traits, 34, 71, 77
Florentine Guelphs, 55, 65
Florio family, 4, 90
Florio, John, 15–16, 33, 43, 50, 56, 57, 68, 83, 85, 90, 92n1
Forcari, Villa (Andrea Palladio), 18
Ford, John, 2
Foscarini, Palazzo, 18
France, 53, 55, 67, 69, 71, 75, 79

France, King of, *AWEW*, 10, 72–6 *passim*
Frederick II, 42
Frederyke of Jennen, 2
Fregosi, 55
'Fynes Moryson, Giordano Bruno and William Shakespeare', 92n28

Galileo, 42
Gascoigne, George, 2, 46, 56, 80
Gaveston, *Edward II*, 79
Genoa, 2, 20, 88
Genoa, Duke of (Prospero Adorno), 5, 83
ghetto (Venice), 21
Gibbons, Brian, 56, 97n54
Gibellines, 55
Gilbert, Allan, 99n27
Giotto, 65
Gismund of Salerne, 2, 91n3
Gl'Ingannati, 3
Globe Theatre, 11
Gobbo, Launcelot, *MV*, 10, 19, 22, 23–4, 25, 89
Gobbo, Old, *MV*, 10, 19, 88
Golding's Ovid, 1
'gondilo', 19
gondolas, 16
'gundolier', 30
Goneril, *KL*, 8
Gonzaga (Mantuan dukes), 3
Gonzago, *H*, 3
Gonzalo, *T*, 69, 83, 84, 86
Gostanzo, *All Fools*, 65
Grand Canal (Venice), 16
Gratiano, *MV*, 17
Gray's Inn, 2
Grazzini, A., 91n2
Gregory XIII, Pope, 81
Gremio, *TS*, 49–51 *passim*, 60
Grillo, E. M., 87, 88
Grindstone, Susan, *RJ*, 57
Grossart, Alexander B., 92n22
Grumio, *TS*, 47, 50, 52
Guarini, 3
Guazzo, Steeven, 48
Gubbio, 15
Guelphs, 55, 65

Index

Guilmartin Jr, John Francis, 95n87, 99n44
Gunpowder and Galleys, 95n87, 99ns44–5
Gunby, D. C., 93n33

Hall, Bishop, 41
Hamlet, 9
Hamlet, *H*, 3, 6, 60
Harington, Sir John, 76
Harris, Bernard, 92n31
Harrison, G. B., 92n33
Harvey, Gabriel, 92n22
Harvey, William, 42
Hatton, Christopher, 91n3
Hecatommithi, 3, 35
Helena, *AWEW*, 10, 41, 71–4 *passim*
Henry VI, Part 1, 8
Henry VI, Part 3, 8
Henry VI plays, 46
Henry VIII, King, 46, 66
Hero, *MAAN*, 7, 10, 77, 78, 79, 82
His Majesties Poetical Exercises at Vacant Houres, 99n48
The History of Italy, 6, 91–9 *passim*
Hoby, Sir Thomas, 40, 79, 89
Hoepfner, Theodore C., 95n103
Holland, Abraham, 80
Holofernes, *LLL*, 3, 12
Holweck, F. G., 99n31
Holy League, 30, 80
homosexuality, 38
The Honest Whore, 2
horses (Naples), 68–9
Hortensio, *TS*, 44, 47, 48, 50, 51, 52
Howard, Clare, 96n9
Hughes, Charles, 92ns25, 11, 96n13, 98n7
Humor Out of Breath, 12
Humphreys, A. R., 77, 99ns33,37,39
'Hundred Merry Tales', 78
Hunter, G. K., 91n1, 92n31, 99ns28–9

I Suppositi, 2

Iago, *O*, 4, 9–10, 16–17, 18, 30–9 *passim*, 58, 82
Iago: Some Approaches to the Illusion of His Motivation, 95n109
'Iago's Nationality', 95n103
Illyria, 1, 11, 66
Imogen, *Cym*, 2
'In Commendation of Musick' (Edwardes), 57
'Induction' to *TS*, 50, 53
Inner Temple, 2
Inquisition, 14, 26
Isabella, *MM*, 3
Islam, 80
Italian
 books, 40, 41
 character, 51
 colour, 4, 11, 16, 19, 30–1, 44, 45, 51–2, 54–6, 62, 87–90 *passim*
 dialect (Florentine), 34
 dowry, 49
 fashions, 4, 6, 13, 16, 21, 41, 51, 57–8, 79
 pedagogy, 50
 poetry, 4
 sources, 2–3, 31, 35, 36, 71, 82, 90
Italian Popular Comedy, 91n10, 100n60
The Italian Renaissance in England, 91ns1,9, 94n59, 96n32, 98n6, 99ns41–2, 100ns6,17
Italica, 91n12, 95n99, 97n39, 99n36
Ithamore, *The Jew of Malta*, 28
Itinerary, An, 71, 92–100 *passim*

Jachimo, *Cym*, 2
Jacobean Theatre, 92n31
James I, King (James VI of Scotland), 5, 14, 43, 81, 82, 86
Jaques, *AYLI*, 5, 51
jealousy, 7, 31, 82
Jeffere, John, 91n2
Jeffrey, Violet M., 87, 93n40, 95n88
Jessica, *MV*, 10, 17, 20, 25
The Jew of Malta, 34
Jewish
 dress, 21
 greed, 22

Jewish – *continued*
  law, 22–3, 26–7
  teaching, 22
  world, 22, 23
  world view, 27
Jews, 9, 16, 17, 21–9 *passim*
John, Don, *MAAN*, 78, 81
John, Don, of Austria, 80–2
John Florio, 93n35, 95n100, 97n38, 100ns57,59, 101ns19–20
John, Friar, *RJ*, 54
John Webster: Three Plays, 93n33
Jonson, Ben, 2, 15–17, 100n61
Joseph, *TS*, 52
Journal of Economic History, 94n60
The Journal of English and Germanic Philology, 91n11, 93n30, 100n15
Julia, *TGV*, 8, 41, 60–4 *passim*
Juliet, *RJ*, 8, 10, 43, 44, 54–60 *passim*, 84
Juriste, *Hecatommithi*, 3

Kate, *TS*, 8, 10, 46–53 *passim*, 72
Kermode, Frank, 69
King John, 8
King Lear, 9

'Lady of Strachy', 88
LaFew, *AWEW*, 72, 74, 75
Lago d'Averno, 67
Lake Campania, 67
La Prima de le Novelle, 76
L'Arcadia, 3
Launce, *TGV*, 61–3 *passim*
Laura (Petrarch's), 55
Lawrence, Friar, *RJ*, 54, 58, 59, 60
'Lazaretto' (*Volpone*: Venice), 16
Lea, K. M., 91n10, 100n60
Leah, *MV*, 17
Leander, 77
learning and education theme, 10, 40–53 *passim*, 58–60, 63–4, 69–77 *passim*, 96n34
Leonato, *MAAN*, 10, 66, 77, 78, 79
Lepanto (James I), 81
Lepanto, Battle of (1571), 30, 80–2
'The Lepanto of James the sixth, King of Scotland', 99n48, 100ns53–4

Lewalski, Barbara, 79
Libre tre, 66
Lightborn, *Edward II*, 68, 85
Lithgow, William, 66
Litio (Hortensio), *TS*, 44, 47
Litio, *Supposes*, 46
Lodge, Thomas, 3
Lodovico, *O*, 30
Lombard region (Lombardy), 43–4, 51–2, 87–8
'Lombard's vinegar', *Volpone*, 16
London, 11, 17, 19, 20, 23, 40, 44, 57, 62, 80–1, 89, 90
Long, Henry, 56
Long, Sir Walter, 56
Lord, *TS*, 50, 53
Lorenzo, *MV*, 22
'lost years', 88
Lotti, Ottaviano, 5
Love's Labour's Lost, 3, 12
Lucentio, *TS*, 9, 10, 41–52 *passim*, 72
Lucetta, *TGV*, 63
Lyly, John, 7, 61, 67

Machiavel, 8, 62, 65
Machiavelli, 4, 8–9, 33, 65, 71, 78
Machiavellian, 8, 22, 35, 62, 65, 73, 84
Machiavelli: The Chief Works and Others, 99n27
The Malcontent, 2
Malevolti, Agnol, *Il Sacrificio*, 3
Malta, 7, 66
Malvolio, *TN*, 3, 11
Manley, Frank, 100n13
Mantua, 2, 9, 41, 44–5, 51, 54, 60, 62
Margaret ('Meg'), *MAAN*, 78, 79
Mariana, *AWEW*, 75
Marlowe, Christopher, 8, 22, 28, 34, 38, 68, 79
marriage customs (Italian), 12
Marston, John, 2, 15, 89
Marx, Robert, 94n85, 99n44
Mary I, Queen, 81
Mary Stuart (of Scots), 42, 81
Massinger, Philip, 2

Index

McKerrow, Ronald B., 92ns29–30, 93n32, 98n19
McWilliams, G. H., 4, 89, 91n15
Measure for Measure, 3, 86
Medici (family), 70–1
Medici, Catherine de, 71
Mercatio, *TGV*, 60
merchant financiers, 21
The Merchant of Venice, 2, 4, 7, 9, 12, 14, 16, 17, 18–29, 30, 46, 66, 68, 87, 88, 90
Mercutio, *RJ*, 57, 58, 59, 60
The Merry Wives of Windsor, 3, 8
Messina, 2, 9, 66, 70, 77–81 *passim*
Milan, 2, 9, 11, 44, 45, 61–2, 63, 67, 69, 83–4, 88
Milan, Duchess of, *MAAN*, 79
Milan, Duke of, 83
Minola, Baptista, *TS*, 10, 49, 50
Miranda, *T*, 10, 69, 70, 83, 84, 86
Modern Language Review, 93n40, 100n7
'Monastery of Augustinian Monkes', 13
'monastery of *San Spiritio*', 16
Montabello, 18
Montague (Montecchi), 56, 80
Montaigne, 15, 83
Moors, 9, 31
More, Sir Thomas, 18
Morocco, Prince of, *MV*, 18, 28
Morris, Brian, 47, 96n31, 97n35
Moryson, Fynes, *passim*
Moryson, Henry, 86
Mosca, *Volpone*, 16
Moth, *LLL*, 3
mountebanks (Venice), 16, 31
Much Ado About Nothing, 2, 7, 66, 76–82
Munday, Anthony, 43, 92n33
Murano, 13

Nanni, 66
Naples, 2, 5, 9, 61, 67–9, 70, 83, 84, 85, 86
Naples, King of (Ferdinando), 83
Narrative and Dramatic Sources of Shakespeare, 91n8, 94n51, 95ns92, 104, 96ns22,31

Nashe, Thomas, 1, 7, 28, 31, 38, 68, 71
Nathaniel, Sir, *LLL*, 3
Naumachia . . ., 80
Navarre, 3
Neapolitans, 67–9
Nelson, Benjamin N., 94n60
Neri, 46, 55
Nerissa, *MV*, 25
Nero and Other Plays, 92n6
The New Arden Editions of Shakespeare's plays
  All's Well That Ends Well, 98ns28–9
  Cymbeline, 91n4
  The Merchant of Venice, 94ns78,81
  Much Ado About Nothing, 99ns33–5,37,39
  Othello, 95n98
  Romeo and Juliet, 97n54
  The Taming of the Shrew, 96ns31,34, 97n35
  The Tempest, 91n18, 98n23, 100ns58,60
  Twelfth Night, 91ns5–7,16
  The Two Gentlemen of Verona, 97ns61–3, 98ns67,70
Nicoll, Allardyce, 91n13, 93n38, 97n43
Nicosia, 29
The Nineteenth Century, 100n16
Noel, Henry, 91n3
Norfolk, *RII*, 12
North, Thomas, 16
Notes and Queries, 92n28, 95n103, 101n18
Nurse, *RJ*, 43, 58, 59, 60

Oatcake, Hugh, *MAAN*, 11, 78
'Old Freetown', *RJ*, 44
Old Testament law, 25
Olivia, *TN*, 11
Oratini Militari, 66
The Orator, Declamation 95, 27
Orlando Furioso, 76
Orsino, Duke, *TN*, 1, 11
Orsino, Don Virginio (Duke of Bracciano), 5
Orthoepia Gallica, 50

Index 109

Othello, 2, 3, 7, 8, 9, 12, 15, 16, 17, 29–39, 58, 68, 77, 85, 87, 90
Othello, O, 7, 10, 17, 28, 30–8 passim, 58, 86
'Othello: The Tragedy of Iago', 95n109
Ottoman, 29–30, 80
Oxford, Earl of (Edward de Vere), 92n22
The Oxford Dictionary of English Christian Names, 99n30
Oxford, University of, 5

PMLA, 99n39, 100n15
Padua (Padoa), 2, 5, 9, 10, 11, 18, 20, 42–53 passim, 61, 63, 77, 88
Paduan, 57
Painter, William, 44, 71
Palladio, Andrea (Villa Forcari), 18
Pallavicino, Lord Gaspare, *Il Cortegiano*, 78
Panthino, *TGV*, 61
Panzodicie, 55
Paradoxes of Defence, 57, 97n59
Paris, 72, 73
Paris, *RJ*, 58, 60
Parks, George B., 91n17, 92ns2–3, 96n17, 98ns3–4
Parolles, *AWEW*, 11, 42, 71–5 passim
Parthenope (Naples), 67
Partridge, A. C., 4, 54, 100n15
Parvis, Henry, 14
Pasha, Mustafa, 29–30
Pasha, Pirali, 29
Il Pastor Fido, 3
Patrick, Friar, *TGV*, 60
Il Pecorone, 18, 20, 26
Pedant, *TS*, 44, 49, 51
Pedro, Don, *MAAN*, 10, 66, 77, 79
'Pegasus' (inn), 89
Peregrine, *Volpone*, 16
Peter, *RJ*, 58
Petrarch, 18, 23, 42, 55
Petruccio (Moryson), 46
Petruchio (name), 46
Petruchio, *Supposes*, 46
Petruchio, *TS*, 10, 46–53 passim, 72
Philaster, 2, 82

Philautus, 61
Philip II, King (Spain), 80, 81
Philip, *TS*, 52
Pisa, 42, 43, 51
Pisan, 52
Pistoia, 46
Pius V, Pope, 80
plague, 88
Plato, 46
The Poems of Shakespeare's Dark Lady, 101n18
poison, 3, 7, 9, 19, 31, 36, 68, 75, 78
political motif in *The Tempest*, 4, 7–8, 10, 84–6
Ponte, Antonio da, 20
Ponte, Jacopo da (Bassano), 18
Pope, 4, 8, 14, 23, 25–6, 28, 55, 66, 67
Pope, Alexander, 52
Porta Nova (Milan), 62
Portia, *MV*, 8, 10, 18–28 passim, 66, 68, 79
Porto, Luigi da, 56
The Posies, 97n55, 99n46
Potpan, Susan, *RJ*, 11, 57
Practice (Saviolo's), 57
Praz, Mario, 4, 18, 54, 66, 100ns4,8
The Prince (Il Principe), 9, 78
Il Principe (The Prince), 8
Prince of Wales (James I's son), 5
Prospero, *T*, 10, 69–70, 83–6 passim
Proteus, *TGV*, 10, 42, 60–4 passim
Prouty, Charles T., 99n33
proverbial phrases, 50
Psychoanalytic Quarterly, 95n109
Purgatorio, 56
Pythagoras, 17

Queen Mab speech, 57

Rafe, *TS*, 52
Raleigh, Sir Walter, 15
Rebeck, Hugh, 57
Red Cross Knight, 24, 74
Regan, *KL*, 8
revenge, 19, 31, 37, 55, 84
The Revenger's Tragedy, 2
Rheims, 47

Rialto, 11, 16, 19–20, 89, 90
Rialto Bridge, 20
Richard II, 12, 38
Richard III, *RIII*; *3HVI*, 8
Riche, Barnabe, 3
Riche his Farewell to Militarie Profession, 3
Rivista di Letterature Moderne e Comparate, 91n11, 96n25, 100n9
Robin Hood, 62
Rocco, Signior, 58
Roderigo, *O*, 17, 30, 37
Roman
  Empire, 67
  religion, 40, 74, 81
Romano, John Christopher, 89
Romano, Julio, 2, 89
Rome, 2, 5, 9, 14, 45, 51, 68, 92n33
Romeo, *RJ*, 10, 41, 43, 44, 54–60 *passim*, 84
Romeo and Juliet, 2, 4, 7, 10, 42, 44, 46, 54–60, 71, 78, 90
Romeus and Juliet, 43–4, 63
Rosalind, *AYLI*, 5
Rosaline, *RJ*, 55, 59
Rosalynde, 3
Rossillion, 72
Rowse, A. L., 101n18

Il Sacrificio, 3
'Sagittary' (inn), 31, 89
'St. Francis' (inn), 72
Saint Gregory's Well (Milan), 11, 62, 88
St. Helena, 74
St. Mark's (Venice), 16, 31
Sandys, George, 20, 66
Sannazaro, Jacapo, 3
Saviolo, Vincentio, 57
Scala, Bartolommeo della, 56
The Scholemaster, 6, 41, 47, 92n7, 94n64, 95ns1–3, 96ns4–8, 97n50, 98n13
Scoto, *Volpone*, 16
Scott, Mary Augusta, 99n39, 100n15
Sea-coal, *MAAN*, 78
Sebastian, *T*, 69, 70, 84, 85

Sebastian, *TN*, 11
Sebastian (Julia), *TGV*, 64
Second Fruites, 15, 16, 43, 50, 68, 93n37
Second Outlaw, *TGV*, 63
The Secondary Heroes of Shakespeare and Other Essays, 97n42
Sells, A. Lytton, 18, 87, 88
Sforza, Duke Ludovico, 67
Sforza, Piero, *Antonio and Mellida* and *Antonio's Revenge*, 15
Sforzas, 89
Shakespeare, possible visit to Italy, 87–90
'Shakespeare and Florence and the Florentines', 3, 95n99, 97n39, 99n36
Shakespeare and Italy, 100ns2–3, 10, 12
'Shakespeare and Italy' (Partridge), 4, 97n45, 100n15
'Shakespeare and Italy' (Simpson), 97n42
'Shakespeare and Italy' (Steer), 101n18
'Shakespeare and the Conversatione', 4
'Shakespeare and the Doge of Venice', 3, 93n30, 94n79, 95n97
'Shakespeare and the Lombard Cities', 3–4, 96n25, 97n41, 100n9
'Shakespeare's Confusion of the two Romanos', 100n15
Shakespeare's Europe, 92–100 *passim*
'Shakespeare's Italy', 4, 92n34, 93n38, 94n52, 97ns43–4, 98n8, 100ns4,8
Shakespeare's Italy Revisited, 4, 91n15, 100n14
Shakespeare-Jahrbuch, 91n11, 94n79
Shakespeare Survey 7, 91n13, 93n38, 97n43, 98n8, 100n4
Shakespeare: The Poet in His World, 97n56
'Shakespeare's Venice', 93n40, 95n88, 100n7

Index

Shakespearian Comedy, 98n71
Shylock, MV, 10, 14, 17, 19, 22–7 passim
Sicilia, 2
Sicilian, 66, 82
Sicily, 2, 66
Siena (Syenna), 55, 65, 71, 74
Sienese Ghibellines, 65
Signory, 40–5, 46, 69
Silver, George, 57–8
Silvia, TGV, 44, 61–4 passim
Simpson, Lucy, 54
Sly, Christopher, TS, 52–3
Smith, Gordon Ross, 95n109
'Some Details of Italian Local Colour in "Othello" ', 3, 94n79, 95n88
Soranzo, Jacopo, 79
Soundpost, James, RJ, 57
The Sources of Much Ado About Nothing, 99n33
Southampton, Earl of, 5, 56–7, 88, 90
Spain, 14, 55, 67, 71, 79, 80, 82
Spanish
  armies, 67
  language, 67
  name (Iago's), 35
  viceroy, 67
'Speculum Tuscanism', 92n22
Speed, TGV, 61–4 passim
La Spiritata, 91n2
Spurio, Captain, AWEW, 72
Stafford, Robert, 91n3
Steer, Barbara D. G., 101n18
Stephano, T, 70, 85
Stillinger, Jack, 96n21
Stirling-Maxwell, William, 99ns49–52
Stoye, John Walter, 9, 38, 93n25, 96n18, 98n1
Stratford, 53
Sullivan, Sir Edward, 89, 97n36
Supposes, 2, 46
Sycorax, 85
Symons, Arthur, 92n6

The Taming of A Shrew, 46

The Taming of the Shrew, 2, 7, 43, 44, 46–53, 58, 60, 72, 87, 88, 89
Tancred and Gismond, 91n3
Tasso, 3, 42
The Tempest, 2, 4, 5–6, 7–8, 10, 11, 67, 69, 70, 82–6, 88–9
terra firma, 9, 12, 40–5, 69, 70
Thames river, 11, 20, 62
Thersites, TC, 68
Third Outlaw, TGV, 60
Thomas, William, 1, 5–6, 9, 12–13, 14, 19, 21, 22, 26, 31, 32, 42, 45, 61–2, 65, 67–8, 71, 76, 79, 83, 90
Thurio, TGV, 63, 64
Tiberio, Captain, 66
Tichfield (Southampton's house), 56
Titus Andronicus, 9, 46
Touring in 1600, 92n26, 93ns26,34, 96n27, 98ns2,9, 100n1
Tourneur, Cyril, 2
tragetto ('traject'), 18, 19, 88
The Tragical History of Romeus and Juliet, 91n3
Tranio, TS, 52
Trattato, 66
travel, see also English travel to Italy
  as educational, 40–2, 50–1, 64
  gambling, 86
Treaty of Granada, 67
Trinculo, T, 85
Tripoli, 51
Troilus, 77
Troilus and Cressida, 9, 68
Turks, 29–30, 31, 32, 80
Tuscan, 16, 31, 72, 73, 78, 79
Tuscany, 5, 34, 65, 66, 71
Twelfth Night, 1, 3, 5, 11, 88
The Two Gentlemen of Verona, 2, 7, 44, 54, 60–4, 83, 88
Tybalt, RJ, 11, 55, 57, 59

Ubaldini, Petruccio, 5, 46, 66
Ulysses, 67
Una (The Faerie Queene), 73
The Unfortunate Traveller, 71, 93n32, 95ns94,108, 98n19

Ursley, *MAAN*, 78
'The Usurer and the Merchant Prince', 94n60
usurers, 21–2

Valentine, *TGV*, 10, 44, 60–4 *passim*
Venetian, *see also* Italian
  ambassador, 42–3, 79
  government, 14–15
  Jews, 21–2
  law, 20–7 *passim*, 33
  'officers of night', 31
  religious freedom, 21–2
  ships, 20–1
  setting, 12–39
  Signory, 40–64
Venetians, 20, 27, 29–31, 32, 35, 39
Venice, 2, 5, 6, 9, 10, 11, 12–39, 40, 42–3, 45, 46, 51, 55, 78, 80, 87–90
Verges, *MAAN*, 78
Verona, 2, 9, 10, 11, 18, 43–4, 45, 49, 52, 53, 54, 56, 59–64 *passim*, 89
Veronese 33, 60–1
  ruins, 44
Vespers Insurrection at Palermo (1283), 66
Vice character, 8
Vincentio, *TS*, 10, 49, 51
Vicenza, 18
Vico, *Hecatommithi*, 3

Vienna, 3
Viola, *TN*, 1, 11
Volpone, 2, 15–17, 46
Volpone, *Volpone*, 16–17

Wangh, Martin, 95n109
wealthy widow, *TS*, 48
Webster, John, 2, 8, 15, 65, 66, 79
Whitebrook, J. C., 92n28
The White Devil, 15, 65, 66
Wilmont, Robert, 91n3
Wilson, F. P., 91n1
Wilson, J. Dover, 97n58
Wilton, Jack, 7, 15, 28, 68
The Winter's Tale, 2
Wittenberg, University of, 6
Wolfe, John, 97n58
The Works of Gabriel Harvey, 921n22
The Works of Thomas Nashe, 92ns29–30, 93n32, 94n82, 95ns94, 108, 98n19
Wotton, Sir Henry, 14, 42–3
Wouldbe, Lady Politic, *Volpone*, 16
Wouldbe, Sir Politic, *Volpone*, 16

Yates, Frances A., 15, 97n38, 100n57, 101ns19–20
Yugoslavia, 1

Zani (Venice: *Volpone*), 16
Zelauto: The Fountaine of Fame, 43, 96n21

Love's vow
CF Sto First #4   T52338

Mediapolis Public Library

Help us Rate this book...
Put your initials on the
Left side and your rating
on the right side.
- 1 = Didn't care for
- 2 = It was O.K.
- 3 = It was great

_____	1 2 3
_____	1 2 3
_____	1 2 3
_____	1 2 3
_____	1 2 3
_____	1 2 3
_____	1 2 3
_____	1 2 3
_____	1 2 3
_____	1 2 3
_____	1 2 3
_____	1 2 3
_____	1 2 3
_____	1 2 3
_____	1 2 3

DATE DUE

FEB 1 6 2021

PRINTED IN U.S.A.

MEDIAPOLIS PUBLIC LIBRARY
128 N. ORCHARD ST.
PO BOX 39
MEDIAPOLIS, IA 52637

© 2017, Melissa Storm

All rights reserved. Except as permitted under the U.S. Copyright Act of 1976, no part of this publication may be reproduced, distributed or transmitted in any form or by any means, or stored in a database or retrieval system without the prior written permission of the publisher.

Editor: Kindle Press
Cover & Graphics Designer: Mallory Rock
Proofreader: Jasmine Bryner

This is a work of fiction. Names, characters, organizations, places, events, and incidents are either products of the author's imagination or are used fictitiously. Any resemblance to actual persons, living or dead, or actual events is purely coincidental.

No part of this work may be reproduced, or stored in a retrieval system, or transmitted in any form or by any means, electronic, mechanical, photocopying, recording, or otherwise, without written permission of the publisher.

Published by Partridge & Pear Press
PO Box 27 | Brighton, MI 48116